PRAYERS

FOR

DIFFICULT

TIMES

FOR

Teen Girls

PRAYERS
FOR
DIFFICULT
TIMES
FOR
Teen Girls

WHEN YOU DON'T KNOW
WHAT TO PRAY

RENAE BRUMBAUGH GREEN

BARBOUR
PUBLISHING

Published by Barbour Publishing, Inc., 1810 Barbour Drive, Uhrichsville, Ohio 44683, www.barbourbooks.com

Our mission is to inspire the world with the life-changing message of the Bible.

Member of the
Evangelical Christian
Publishers Association

Printed in the United States of America.

CONTENTS

INTRODUCTION

For you have been my hope, Sovereign
Lord, my confidence since my youth.

PSALM 71:5 NIV

. . . .

The teen years are an exciting, frustrating time.
It felt that way for your grandmother. And your
mother. Now you're living it, and you may feel like
nobody understands.

And you may be right.

After all, your mom didn't grow up with social
media. Your grandmother didn't have 24-hour access
to all the bad things her parents warned against.
People didn't laugh at them for wanting to follow
God and make good choices.

Or did they? They may not have had a cell phone
or the Internet, but those who wanted to follow God
have always faced hard times. The good news is that
God is the same yesterday, today, and forever. He'll
never make light of your problems or ignore your
request for wisdom. Nothing you face, nothing you
say surprises Him. He loves you more than He loves
His own life. He invites you to tell Him everything.
He'll always listen, without harsh judgment. He'll
hold you through the worst of the storm, dry your
tears, and set you on the right path.

All you have to do is talk to Him.

ABUSE

Vindicate the weak and fatherless;
do justice to the afflicted and destitute.
PSALM 82:3 NASB

. . . .

Dear Father, I know You are not an abusive Father, and mistreatment of any kind makes You angry. I don't understand why You allow people to be abused. It seems like evil, cruel people get away with such horrible things. But I know You are good. I know You are kind. And I know You love justice. Help me trust You even when I don't understand. Help me take a stand against abuse, whether I'm the one being abused or it's someone I know. Give me wisdom for when to speak, when to act, and when to wait. Place trustworthy people in my life that I can share my concerns with. Most of all, Father, make good on Your promises to vindicate the weak, to bring justice to the afflicted, and to defend the powerless.

*For God has not given us a spirit of timidity,
but of power and love and discipline.*
2 TIMOTHY 1:7 NASB

. . . .

Dear Father, thank You for this reminder that
You created me to be powerful and strong.
Satan wants me to be afraid. He wants me to
be timid. He wants me to operate from anxiety
and from a belief that I'm powerless. But You
make me powerful! When people are abusive,
they prey on others' fears. That's not from You,
and it's not who You are. It can be hard to separate those fears from reality, those lies from
the truth. When others abuse me, remind me
of who I am in You. When the voices in my head
repeat abusive beliefs, remind me that those are
lies. Speak Your truth into my life: I am strong
through Jesus Christ. I am powerful because You
live in me. I am loving, and love conquers all.
You made me more than a conqueror through
Christ.

*Fathers, do not provoke your children
to anger, but bring them up in the
discipline and instruction of the Lord.*
EPHESIANS 6:4 NASB

. . . .

Dear Father, thank You for being a kind, wise, loving Father. I know You're cheering for my success. You never insult me or remind me of my failures. My own parents, and other authority figures in my life, are only human. Sometimes, they're unkind. Sometimes, they even treat me unfairly. When I feel mistreated, remind me that it's coming from a flawed person, not from You. Protect me when I need protection. Remind me that harsh words are a reflection of others' fears and anxieties, not a reflection of Your love for me. Teach me the balance of showing respect and tolerating tough love. Give me wisdom, and when appropriate, lead me to trustworthy adults I can talk to. Keep me safe, and help me never abuse anyone else.

The mouth of the righteous is a fountain of life,
but the mouth of the wicked conceals violence.
PROVERBS 10:11 NASB

. . . .

Dear Father, in this age of social media, everyone puts on a front. They post pictures of a posed, perfect life. But those pictures don't always reflect the truth. I'm just as guilty as anyone. I share the pretty parts of my life, but I conceal the ugly parts. Give me wisdom, Lord. It's hard to understand the difference between what's on the surface and what lies beneath. Help me see those around me who are hurting, who might be victims of abuse. Show me how to help them. Lead me to adults I can trust, and give me wisdom about when and what to share. Finally, help me to never be the abusive one— ever. Make my words and actions a fountain of life, flowing Your love to those around me.

"See that you do not look down on one of these little ones; for I say to you that their angels in heaven continually see the face of My Father who is in heaven."
MATTHEW 18:10 NASB

. . . .

Dear Father, You are strong. You are powerful. Yet You never use that power against the weak or the innocent. Instead, You guard and protect children, and You defend those without defense. You are never the villain, always the hero. Sometimes, I feel abused, Father. Save me. Protect me. Remove me from abusive situations, or prevent my abuser from being able to act. Make me wise and strong—like You, Father. Help me defend myself as You defend me. Remind me that having love and humility doesn't mean I must accept abuse. This verse suggests I have angels fighting for me; strengthen them as You strengthen me. Please make it stop. Thank You for defending me.

ADDICTION

No temptation has overtaken you except something common to mankind; and God is faithful, so He will not allow you to be tempted beyond what you are able, but with the temptation will provide the way of escape also, so that you will be able to endure it. Therefore, my beloved, flee from idolatry.
1 CORINTHIANS 10:13–14 NASB

. . . .

Dear Father, when it comes to addiction, most people think of drugs or alcohol. But anything that controls me, that takes over my thoughts and dictates my actions, is an addiction. I can be addicted to my phone, television, unhealthy food, and many other things. You know my heart, my weaknesses, and my tendencies. Help me overcome my addictions. I know You understand what it's like to be tempted. I also know You make me strong. When I call on You, You'll provide a way for me to escape the temptation in that moment. Give me the strength, self-discipline, and desire to conquer the things that control me.

Do not be deceived: "Bad company
corrupts good morals."
1 CORINTHIANS 15:33 NASB

· ·

Dear Father, I like my friends. I enjoy fitting in and feeling accepted. But sometimes I let their opinions dictate my behavior. Their attitudes influence my thoughts more than I want to admit. I recognize that I have some addictions I need to deal with, and some of my friends don't understand or support my struggle. By spending time with people who have different goals and values, I make it harder for myself. My chances of overcoming my addictions are higher if I surround myself with people who support my goals. Help me choose friends wisely. Send new, godly, supportive friends my way, and help me distance myself from those who sabotage my goals. Give me strength not to run back to what is comfortable. Surround me with people who will encourage me, support me, and pray for me in this journey.

*All things are permitted for me, but not all
things are of benefit. All things are permitted
for me, but I will not be mastered by anything.*
1 CORINTHIANS 6:12 NASB

. . . .

Dear Father, it's interesting that Paul says nothing is off-limits as long as it doesn't control him. I know he's not talking about things You've already labeled as sinful. But there are some gray areas, like phone use and social media. It's fine for me to have these things as long as they don't dominate my thoughts and control my life. I can think of other examples too. . .but the point is, anything that controls me, other than You, is an addiction. If something threatens to take over my thoughts and dictate my actions, help me avoid it. I only want to be addicted to You—to Your goodness, Your kindness, Your grace. Fill me with Your presence so completely that everything else is crowded out.

Submit therefore to God. But resist the devil, and he will flee from you.
JAMES 4:7 NASB

. . . .

Dear Father, Satan wants to destroy me and keep me from living the abundant, purpose-filled life You have planned for me. He wants me to be addicted to things that aren't good for me. He throws temptation my way every chance he gets. He whispers into my thoughts and makes me want things that will destroy me. But I want Your plans for my life, Lord, not Satan's. When I face temptation, remind me of the strength You've placed inside me. Help me say no to the things that will destroy me. Christ is called the Lion of Judah. . .Remind me of that picture of You, as a roaring Lion, whenever I feel weak. I know You are with me always, and Your presence makes me strong.

"Call upon Me on the day of trouble;
I will rescue you, and you will honor Me."
PSALM 50:15 NASB

. . . .

Dear Father, I know You always hear me when I call. But this verse says You'll do more than just listen. You'll actually rescue me. I need rescuing, Lord. The desire for the thing that controls me is strong, and I feel weak. I've already stumbled so many times on this journey. I really need Your help, Lord. I'm calling on You right now, claiming Your promise to deliver me safely out of my addiction. I know You're using this situation to make me stronger and to prepare me for a bigger purpose and plan than I can imagine. Remind me not to worry about tomorrow or next week or even what will happen in one hour. Deliver me right now from the need for my addiction. Distract me. Make me strong. Help me through this present crisis.

ALCOHOL / DRUG USE

*And do not get drunk with wine, for that is
debauchery; but be filled with the Spirit.*
Ephesians 5:18 RSV

. . . .

Dear Father, many of my friends drink alcohol
and use drugs. They act like it's no big deal, like
it's a rite of passage for people my age. On the
surface, it can seem harmless and fun. But when
I look a little closer, I really can't find anything
good that comes from underage drinking or
illegal drug use. It lowers defenses and makes
people do things they wouldn't normally do if
they were sober. It puts the person and those
around them in danger by encouraging reckless
behavior. It increases the risk of addiction and
makes it more difficult to achieve success. Help
me stand strong against alcohol and drug use.
Instead, fill me with Your Holy Spirit. Make me
an example of how to have joy, peace, and lots
of fun without those things.

Wine is a mocker, strong drink a brawler;
and whoever is led astray by it is not wise.
PROVERBS 20:1 RSV

. . . .

Dear Father, I've been mocked before. It feels terrible to have others make fun of me in a mean way. Alcohol and drugs mock people by encouraging them to do things they know are wrong or foolish. Then, when they have to deal with the consequences of that behavior, alcohol and drugs can't help them. Sometimes, I feel like I'd be more accepted or more popular if I drink and do drugs, but I know that kind of acceptance is temporary. It will only end up making me feel worse about myself and my life. Give me wisdom and strength to avoid that behavior. Give me courage to say no. Send me friends who will accept me and encourage me to live a wise, godly life.

*Be sober, be watchful. Your adversary
the devil prowls around like a roaring
lion, seeking some one to devour.*
1 PETER 5:8 RSV

. . . .

Dear Father, the first words of this verse say it all. *Be sober.* You created our minds and our bodies with such precision, and they're designed to work well under Your guidance. When we mess with our brains through inappropriate use of drugs and alcohol, we invite weakness. We invite Satan to take advantage of that weakness to destroy the good plans You have for our lives. I know You can overcome any bad situation and turn it around for good, but I'd rather avoid the bad situations in the first place. Satan wants me to think Your ways are restrictive and punishing, but I know Your wisdom makes me strong and propels me into my best life. Make me wise, keep me sober, and help me watch out for Satan's plans to mess up my life.

Who has woe? Who has sorrow? Who has strife? Who has complaining? Who has wounds without cause? Who has redness of eyes? Those who tarry long over wine, those who go to try mixed wine.
PROVERBS 23:29–30 RSV

Dear Father, the things I see on television and social media often make it look like alcohol and drugs lead to a better life. Pictures of laughing, beautiful people holding beer cans, bonding with each other through drug use. . .Those aren't accurate portrayals, are they? The true picture is of someone vomiting over a toilet, sitting in a hospital room after an accident, re-evaluating their life plans because of some foolish choice made while drunk or high. Thank You for Your warnings about such behavior. I know You love me and only want the best for my life. Help me avoid the sorrow that often comes with alcohol and drug abuse.

Do not look at wine when it is red,
when it sparkles in the cup and goes
down smoothly. At the last it bites like
a serpent, and stings like an adder.
PROVERBS 23:31–32 RSV

. . . .

Dear Father, sometimes, alcohol does taste sweet and sugary, and it seems innocent enough. In the beginning, drug and alcohol use can feel like a potion that makes people forget all their troubles. But it's a trick, isn't it? It's all an illusion. The more people use drugs and alcohol to forget their problems, the more troubles they end up having. It doesn't take long before they crave those substances at the first sign of stress, and they need that drink or that smoke to help them relax. Eventually, they require more and more to do the same thing, and that behavior spirals into even bigger problems. Give me wisdom, courage, and strength to say no to the first taste.

ANGER

*Know this, my beloved brethren. Let every
man be quick to hear, slow to speak,
slow to anger, for the anger of man does
not work the righteousness of God.*
JAMES 1:19–20 RSV

Dear Father, why is it that what comes naturally is usually the opposite of what You want me to do? You want me to be slow to anger, but lately it seems anger boils just below my surface. I don't know why I'm so moody, but it doesn't take much to make me want to explode. Sometimes, I have a legitimate reason to be angry. Other times, I just want to be left alone. Forgive me for getting angry so easily. Give me Your peace. Fill me with Your Holy Spirit, and control my reactions. Thank You for Your patience and love toward me. Help me show the same kind of patience and love to those around me.

A fool gives full vent to his anger,
but a wise man quietly holds it back.
PROVERBS 29:11 RSV

. . . .

Dear Father, sometimes, I have legitimate reasons to be angry. Even then, I know it's not wise to explode with whatever comes into my mind at that moment. It's always better to take some deep breaths and really think through what I want to say to others. Once I say something in anger, I can't take it back. I can apologize, but my words will live in that person's memory for the rest of his or her life. When I'm angry, give me wisdom. Fill my heart with Your love, and help me treat others with patience and kindness—even when they don't deserve it—because that's how You treat me. Give me strength to hold back my anger, and help me measure my words before I speak.

Good sense makes a man slow to anger,
and it is his glory to overlook an offense.
PROVERBS 19:11 RSV

. . . .

Dear Father, fools don't have good sense, and their actions lead to all kinds of problems. One of the most obvious signs of foolish behavior is getting angry at every little thing. Those people often end up lonely and bitter because no one wants to be around them. I don't want to be foolish, Lord. Help me be more laid-back so things don't upset me so easily. When someone does something to upset me, help me know when to keep it to myself. I don't want others pointing out everything I do wrong, so I know I shouldn't do that to them. All of this makes sense when I talk to You, Father, but it's harder when I'm dealing with people who annoy me. Give me good sense and make me wise, patient, and kind.

Be angry, and do not sin; ponder in your own hearts on your beds, and be silent.
PSALM 4:4 ESV

. . . .

Dear Father, thank You for this reminder that it's okay to be angry sometimes. Jesus got angry in the temple. That was an appropriate time to be angry because people were taking advantage of the poor in Your name. Most of the time when I feel angry, it's because my pride is hurt or someone just annoys me. Give me wisdom to know how to handle my anger. If it's something small, teach me coping strategies so I don't say and do things I'll regret. But if someone is being hurt or taken advantage of, give me wisdom for how to respond. Show me how to use appropriate anger in a way that honors You, protects the innocent, and shines Your love in a dark world.

ANXIETY / FEAR / WORRY

Fear not, for I am with you, be not dismayed, for I am your God; I will strengthen you, I will help you, I will uphold you with my victorious right hand.
ISAIAH 41:10 RSV

. . . .

Dear Father, some days I'm afraid of everything. I can't even put a name to my fears. I just know that deep inside, I'm anxious. I worry I'll say or do the wrong thing. I worry about what others think of me. I worry about all kinds of things that may never happen. But fear isn't from You, is it? Fear is the belief that something bad will happen. It's the opposite of hope, which is the belief that good things are in store. You are the God of hope. You promise to stay with me, to give me strength, and to hold my hand. When I feel afraid, remind me that I'm strong, I'm not alone, and I belong to You.

"Have I not commanded you? Be strong and courageous. Do not be afraid; do not be discouraged, for the LORD your God will be with you wherever you go."
JOSHUA 1:9 NIV

. . . .

Dear Father, sometimes, the fear in my head is so loud I can't hear anything else. But this verse isn't a suggestion. It's not an inspirational pep talk. It's a command! I'm Your child, and I'm not supposed to be afraid. Instead, You created me to be strong. To be courageous. To be victorious. You made me in Your image, which means I'm fierce. I'm more than a conqueror. You gave me these orders: Don't be afraid. Don't be discouraged. You followed up these commands with a promise that I'm never alone. You, the God of the universe, the all-powerful King of kings, are with me wherever I go. Remind me of this command today, and let me feel Your presence.

When I am afraid, I put my trust in you.
PSALM 56:3 NIV

. . . .

Dear Father, I'm glad it's not a sin to be afraid. Fear is a natural human emotion. I don't have to be ashamed of my fear. Instead, I need to direct that fear to the right place—to You. While it's not a sin to be afraid, it is a sin to *wallow* in fear. I'm supposed to trust You with that fear. Help me understand the difference. Give me the self-discipline to place my fear in Your hands and leave it there. Teach me to trust in You. I know when I trust You, You'll replace my fear with Your peace. Even if the fear comes back again and again, remind me to transfer it to You every single time. Remind me to *trust* You every single time. I know You'll replace my worries with Your peace, every single time.

*Do not be anxious about anything, but in
every situation, by prayer and petition,
with thanksgiving, present your requests
to God. And the peace of God, which
transcends all understanding, will guard
your hearts and your minds in Christ Jesus.*
PHILIPPIANS 4:6–7 NIV

• •

Dear Father, thank You for giving me detailed
instructions for what to do with my anxiety.
When I feel anxious, I'm supposed to pray. You're
not shocked or angry about anything I share.
As I pray, You want me to think of all the things
I'm thankful for. Those thoughts of gratitude
act like a disinfectant, killing the germs of fear.
You invite me to tell You anything, to ask You
for anything. Every time I do this, by the end
of our conversation, I feel Your peace. Thank
You for this formula to get rid of anxiety. I trust
You completely.

*For the Spirit God gave us does
not make us timid, but gives us
power, love and self-discipline.*
2 TIMOTHY 1:7 NIV

. . . .

Dear Father, some days I feel powerful and strong, like I can do anything. But sometimes I just want to stay in bed and pull the covers over my head. Sometimes, this world feels too much for me, and I want to hide. But You didn't make me to be timid, did You? You made me in Your powerful image. You made me strong. You made me loving, even when love is hard. You made me self-controlled, even when negative emotions and desires try to control me. When I feel weak and afraid, remind me of who I am in You. Remind me that I'm Your child, and I've inherited Your traits of power, love, and self-control. You are the Lion of Judah, and I walk beside You, with the authority of a king's daughter.

ARGUMENTS

Do everything without grumbling or arguing.
PHILIPPIANS 2:14 NIV

. . . .

Dear Father, do You really mean *everything*? Like, all the things? I'm never supposed to grumble or complain or argue at all, ever? That goes against everything in my human nature. But I know You're right. Grumbling under my breath about things I don't like doesn't improve the situation. It only makes things worse. And arguing rarely (if ever) changes the other person's mind. It only makes everyone angrier and causes people to be defensive. Teach me to edit my words before they come out of my mouth. If my thoughts are negative, help me keep them to myself and only discuss them with You. Let every word I speak be kind and encouraging. Give me patience and self-discipline to push negative thoughts and speech aside and replace them with Your amazing, overwhelming love.

Keep reminding God's people of these things. Warn them before God against quarreling about words; it is of no value, and only ruins those who listen.
2 TIMOTHY 2:14 NIV

. . . .

Dear Father, I don't mean to be argumentative. But sometimes people annoy me, and I feel like I have to say something. People make me angry, and I want to pick a fight. Or someone else picks a fight with me, and I feel the need to defend myself. Although an argument may feel right in the moment, it only causes damage. If I need to discuss something with someone, help me do so calmly, with patience, kindness, and love. Help me listen more than I speak and help me understand the other person's point of view, even if I disagree. Give me wisdom to know when an argument is pointless, and help me walk away without comment. I want all my words and actions to be a reflection of Your love.

Don't have anything to do with foolish and stupid arguments, because you know they produce quarrels. And the Lord's servant must not be quarrelsome but must be kind to everyone, able to teach, not resentful.
2 TIMOTHY 2:23–24 NIV

. . . .

Dear Father, it's easy to get sucked into those foolish, stupid arguments. . .the ones where nobody wins and everybody ends up crying or mad. Help me keep my mouth shut, Lord! Help me replace mean words with kind ones. Instead of tearing down, help me build others up. This is one of the hardest things I deal with, because I always want to have the last word or prove I'm right. But that behavior isn't fitting for a child of the King. You want me to be gracious and kind to everyone so they'll see the family resemblance and understand that You're gracious and kind. Give me strength to avoid arguments. Make me a reflection of Your love.

*. . .to be obedient, to be ready to do
whatever is good, to slander no one,
to be peaceable and considerate, and
always to be gentle toward everyone.*
TITUS 3:1–2 NIV

. . . .

Dear Father, this is a pretty ambitious list of traits You want me to carry. But I know each characteristic holds great purpose. Each quality helps me become more of the person You created me to be. When I'm obedient, I show that I trust You. When I'm ready to do what is good, it shows I want to serve You. You don't want me to gossip. Instead, You want me to live at peace with others. You want me to be kind, considerate, and gentle to everyone. These traits are actually Your traits. By living them out, I show the world who You are. Help me control my anger, avoid arguments, and show Your love to everyone I meet.

BETRAYAL

Even my close friend in whom I trusted, who
ate my bread, has lifted his heel against me.
PSALM 41:9 ESV

• •

Dear Father, David wrote these words when he felt betrayed by people he thought he could trust. They gossiped and whispered about him and imagined the worst for him. At that point in his life, he was innocent. He hadn't done anything except try to follow You. Betrayal hurts, Lord. It cuts like a knife, deep and piercing. Like David, I know I can come to You with that pain, and You'll always listen. You're always on my side. And as I read further in this chapter, I see that in spite of the pain, David found joy and peace in You. Help me find that same comfort in Your presence. Use this situation to teach me love, kindness, and loyalty. May I never cause the kind of pain that others have caused me.

David went out to meet them and said to them, "If you have come to me in friendship to help me, my heart will be joined to you; but if to betray me to my adversaries, although there is no wrong in my hands, then may the God of our fathers see and rebuke you."

1 CHRONICLES 12:17 ESV

. . . .

Dear Father, David didn't know who to trust. Because a few people had betrayed him, he could have held everyone at a distance. But he didn't reject everyone because of the actions of a few. He continued to trust, continued to accept friendship where it was offered. He prayed for wisdom, and he trusted You with the outcome. Help me follow David's example. Give me wisdom about who to trust and who to avoid. When others betray me, I know You see it all, and You'll take care of things so I don't have to.

*It is better to take refuge in the
LORD than to trust in man.*
PSALM 118:8 ESV

. . . .

Dear Father, I trusted people. I trusted them with my whole heart, and they hurt me. They betrayed me, and I'm left feeling alone and confused. Why didn't I see? Why didn't I protect myself better? I'm broken, Father, and I don't know how to respond. But I know deep in my pain is a lesson: people will always let me down because no one is perfect. You, on the other hand, will never let me down. You are only love, and You love me fiercely. You love me with a force I can't even imagine. Be my safe place, Lord. Help me love others and trust You. Give me wisdom about who to trust and when so that I don't go through this pain again.

*"But behold, the hand of him who
betrays me is with me on the table."*
LUKE 22:21 ESV

. . . .

Dear Father, Jesus understood what it felt like to be betrayed by a dear friend. Judas was one of His inner circle. They traveled together, played together, worked together, prayed together. And yet, betrayal didn't take Jesus by surprise. He was hurt, but He didn't let it destroy Him. Instead, He trudged forward with strength and courage, head held high, knowing none of it took You by surprise either. It was all part of Your plan. I know that, somehow, this pain I feel is part of Your plan for me too. Somehow, You'll use this to make me more like You. Just as Jesus was victorious over sin and death, I know I'll be victorious over this. Give me strength, wisdom, and grace to keep moving forward.

Faithful are the wounds of a friend;
profuse are the kisses of an enemy.
PROVERBS 27:6 ESV

. . . .

Dear Father, sometimes it's hard to tell who is for me and who is against me. People who care about me will sometimes tell me things I don't want to hear, and it can feel like a betrayal. Others may tell me exactly what I want to hear, but they don't really care about my future or my well-being. Give me wisdom to know who to trust and who to listen to. Show me who loves me and has my best interest at heart and who just wants to manipulate me. When those who care about me tell me things I don't like, help me listen anyway. Teach me to recognize my true friends and trust their "wounds." Help me apply those things to my life that will make me stronger, wiser, and more like You.

BITTERNESS

See to it that no one fails to obtain the grace of God; that no "root of bitterness" springs up and causes trouble, and by it many become defiled.
HEBREWS 12:15 ESV

. . . .

Dear Father, when a root springs up beneath the ground, it spreads. At first, it may not be visible above the surface, but it's there, wrapping its tendrils around everything nearby. By the time it breaks ground and becomes visible, it's really hard to get rid of it. It has already taken over. Bitterness is just that kind of root. At first, I can paint on a smile and pretend everything is okay, but inside, that bitterness wraps around every part of me. I know if I don't deal with it now, it will eventually destroy me. Help me forgive. Help me let go of past hurts. Give me wisdom and peace, and help me leave those hurts in Your hands so I can be free.

Who is wise and understanding among you?
By his good conduct let him show his works
in the meekness of wisdom. But if you have
bitter jealousy and selfish ambition in your
hearts, do not boast and be false to the truth.
JAMES 3:13–14 ESV

. . . .

Dear Father, it's interesting that You paint wisdom and understanding in contrast to bitterness, jealousy, and selfishness. I want to be wise. I want to see things the way You see them. But wisdom requires humility, and humility requires an honest admission of my faults. The truth is, I'm jealous sometimes. I want what others have, whether it's friends or money or status or physical appearance. I want to be the best, and I'm frustrated when others outshine me. But that leads to bitterness, and that's not who I want to be. Help me be happy for others' blessings without comparing myself to them. Make me wise, and teach me to love.

When my soul was embittered, when I was
pricked in heart, I was brutish and ignorant;
I was like a beast toward you.
Nevertheless, I am continually with
you; you hold my right hand.
PSALM 73:21–23 ESV

. . . .

Dear Father, bitterness turns us into monsters, doesn't it? When I feel angry inside, when I hold on to past hurts and think about them often, I'm less attractive. Others don't want to be around me when I'm bitter, and that makes me even angrier. Yet even when I'm at my worst, I know You love me. Even at my worst, You never leave me. You stay right beside me, holding my hand and pulling me toward You. I don't want to carry around this anger anymore. But the roots run deep, and I don't know how to let go. Please take this from me. Today, I'll give You what I can, and tomorrow I'll give You more. Thank You for loving me.

Behold, it was for my welfare that I had great bitterness; but in love you have delivered my life from the pit of destruction, for you have cast all my sins behind your back.
ISAIAH 38:17 ESV

. . . .

Dear Father, there are things in my past that I have a right to be angry about. People have wronged me, and life hasn't been kind. I may have a right to hold on to that anger, but I know it won't do me any good. Bitterness is a cruel master, and it makes me a slave. You came to set me free, but I have to let go of my anger. I have to let go of past hurts and let You handle them. I know You will bring justice in Your time. Until then, help me rest in the freedom of Your love.

*"Beware lest there be among you a man
or woman or clan or tribe whose heart is
turning away today from the LORD our God
to go and serve the gods of those nations.
Beware lest there be among you a root
bearing poisonous and bitter fruit."*
DEUTERONOMY 29:18 ESV

. . . .

Dear Father, bitterness is a poison, and it starts with turning away from You, just a little bit. I'm angry, and I pretend not to be. But inside, I choose not to forgive. Or I'm upset that something didn't go my way. I pretend I don't care, but inside, it eats away at me. When I choose to hang on to anger, frustration, or bitterness, I choose my will over Yours. Before I know it, bitterness has consumed me, destroyed my peace, and killed my joy. Help me release my anger and bitterness to You, Father. Pull me close. Teach me to let go and trust You completely.

BULLYING

*For the ruthless will come to an end and the
scorner will be finished, indeed all who are
intent on doing evil will be eliminated.*
ISAIAH 29:20 NASB

. . . .

Dear Father, thank You for this reminder that
You see all. You know all. And You will not let the
wicked go unpunished. It's not my job to seek
revenge—You'll take care of that. Please protect
me from those who bully me, who are mean and
cruel and say awful things. Hide me from them
when possible. And when I must face them, help
me do it with wisdom and courage. Give me
strength to be kind without being a doormat.
Surround me with friends who will encourage
me and stand beside me no matter what, and
help me be that kind of friend to others. No
matter what happens, make me a reflection of
Your love to those who don't know You.

*"Blessed are those who have been
persecuted for the sake of righteousness,
for theirs is the kingdom of heaven."*
MATTHEW 5:10 NASB

. . . .

Dear Father, I know there are many different levels of persecution, and You recognize all of them. You hate it when Your children suffer for doing right and for honoring You. Right now, I feel bullied. I feel persecuted, when I haven't done anything to deserve it. And according to this verse, I'm blessed, and I will be rewarded for my troubles. But I don't feel blessed. I'm so grateful for Your promises, Father. But I need You to act right here, right now. I need You to intervene. Protect me from cruel people. Surround me with others who will support me. Show me how to respond to mean, bullying people in a way that pleases You. Make me brave. Make me wise. And make me a window of Your love for everyone to see.

"Blessed are you when people insult you and persecute you, and falsely say all kinds of evil against you because of Me."

MATTHEW 5:11 NASB

. . . .

Dear Father, wow. This verse almost makes me laugh. Blessed when people insult me? I don't feel blessed at all. In fact, it feels pretty rotten to be bullied, to have people say terrible things about me and laugh at my expense. I guess the blessing is hidden somewhere. I'm confident You will use this situation to make me stronger, kinder, and wiser. I know for certain I don't want to ever cause another human to feel the pain I feel now. Make it stop, Father. But also, use this situation to make me more like You. I know love conquers all, so take these hateful circumstances and use them to explode Your love in my life.

Therefore I delight in weaknesses, in insults, in distresses, in persecutions, in difficulties, in behalf of Christ; for when I am weak, then I am strong.
2 CORINTHIANS 12:10 NASB

Dear Father, Paul used some pretty intense language here. He delights in insults and persecutions? That's crazy. But as I read deeper, I see he's not saying that he likes being bullied. He's acknowledging that the harder the things get, the more You show up. The weaker we become, the more You flex Your muscles. I need You to flex Your muscles in my life now, Father. I'm feeling pretty weak and beaten down, and I don't know how much more I can take. Make me strong. Be strong in me. Protect me, and get me through this situation quickly. Thank You for being my defender when I can't defend myself.

"For in the way you judge, you will be judged; and by your standard of measure, it will be measured to you."
MATTHEW 7:2 NASB

. . . .

Dear Father, right now, I feel like everyone I know is judging me. Their judgments are harsh and unfair, and I just want to sink into the earth and hide. But I know You see it all. I know You'll take care of me, and You'll see that justice is done. Help me resist the temptation to return cruelty with cruelty. I know that, no matter how mean others are, I don't need to behave like them. Help me love my enemies and leave the judgment to You. Protect me. Stop the bullying, the gossip, and the vicious rumors and actions. Make me brave, strong, and wise, and surround me with other brave, strong, wise people. Please bring a quick end to my situation.

CHALLENGES

Beloved, do not be surprised at the fiery ordeal among you, which comes upon you for your testing, as though something strange were happening to you; but to the degree that you share the sufferings of Christ, keep on rejoicing, so that at the revelation of His glory you may also rejoice and be overjoyed.
1 PETER 4:12–13 NASB

. . . .

Dear Father, life takes me by surprise sometimes, and I don't know how to react. Often, my first response is to ask, "Why me?" We live in a broken world where bad things happen, and no one is immune. You've already blessed me beyond measure with Your gift of salvation. In my lifetime, I know I'll experience joy and hardship. As much as I love the joy, I know it's usually the hardship that makes me more like You. Help me rejoice when I face challenges, because that's when I know You're doing important work in my life.

*In this you greatly rejoice, even though now
for a little while, if necessary, you have been
distressed by various trials, so that the proof
of your faith, being more precious than
gold which perishes though tested by fire,
may be found to result in praise, glory, and
honor at the revelation of Jesus Christ.*
1 PETER 1:6-7 NASB

. . . .

Dear Father, gold is beautiful, shiny, and costly. But it's pretty useless in its raw form. In order to be useful, it must be refined. Refining is a difficult procedure that separates the bad stuff from the pure gold. It's only after the refining process that the gold becomes useful. When I face challenges, remind me that I'm valuable. But I'm not as useful as I can be yet. Each challenge, each hardship I face, refines me and makes me more useful. Thank You for the challenges that make me more like You.

We are afflicted in every way, but not crushed;
perplexed, but not despairing; persecuted, but
not abandoned; struck down, but not destroyed.
2 CORINTHIANS 4:8–9 NASB

. . . .

Dear Father, You really did create us in Your image, didn't You? You are powerful, and I carry that power inside of me. You are almighty, and I have great strength as well—even more than I realize. Satan wants me to doubt myself and question my ability to withstand hardship. He uses other people's opinions of me, and even my own thoughts, against me. When I feel like life is too much, remind me that You live inside me and that nothing is too big for You. Because of You, I am more than a conqueror. Because of You, at the end of it all, I will still stand. No matter what challenges I face, I'll face them with Your strength.

Blessed is a man who perseveres under trial; for once he has been approved, he will receive the crown of life which the Lord has promised to those who love Him.
JAMES 1:12 NASB

• •

Dear Father, I once heard a teacher say she didn't *give* grades; her students *earned* grades. They earned *good* grades by studying, paying attention in class, and turning in assignments. In the same way, I guess You don't pass out those impressive crowns for free. We have to earn them by consistently following You. I can't earn salvation—that was a gift. But when I make difficult choices to obey You even when it's hard, I know those choices help me become the best version of who You created me to be. Help me stand strong when I face trials. I want to please You. I want to earn that crown of life You give to those who follow You.

DEPRESSION

*When the righteous cry for help, the L*ORD
hears and delivers them out of all their troubles.
*The L*ORD *is near to the brokenhearted*
and saves the crushed in spirit.
PSALM 34:17–18 ESV

. . . .

Dear Father, You said when Your people cry for help, You'll hear, and You'll deliver them. *I'm crying out.* You said You're close to the brokenhearted. *That's me.* You said You save those whose spirits are crushed. *That's where I am right now, Lord.* Every part of me—mind, soul, and spirit—feels broken. I'm sad. I want to stay in bed and cry all the time. This life just seems so long, and it feels too much for me right now. Can You please help me? Send me friends. Do what it takes to pull me out of this depression. Help me find my joy again.

Answer me quickly, O Lord! My spirit fails!
Hide not your face from me, lest I be like
those who go down to the pit. Let me hear
in the morning of your steadfast love, for
in you I trust. Make me know the way I
should go, for to you I lift up my soul.
PSALM 143:7–8 ESV

• •

Dear Father, David may have written these words, but they could have come from me. My spirit fails, and I feel like You've hidden Your face from me. I need to know You're near. I need You to show Yourself. I've lost my will and my way, and I need You to help me out of this depression. Show me what to do. I'll try anything—I'll exercise, I'll eat different things—whatever it takes to pull me out of this dark place, I'll do it. Help me. Let me feel Your presence. Let me experience Your joy again.

"The thief comes only to steal and kill and destroy. I came that they may have life and have it abundantly."
JOHN 10:10 ESV

. . . .

Dear Father, where is that abundant life You promised? Where is the peace, the joy, and the overcoming spirit You said were a part of my inheritance? Satan—the thief—has stolen it. He's killed my happiness and destroyed my spirit. But You can restore. You can heal. I know You love me, and You don't want me to live this way. Rescue me, Father. Pull me out of this depression. Give me wisdom for what I can do to conquer this. I know healing may take time, but I trust You. I know You are working on my behalf. One day, I'll smile again. One day, I'll laugh. And one day soon, I'll feel joy, and I'll know You are fighting to give me the abundant life You promised.

"You keep him in perfect peace whose mind is stayed on you, because he trusts in you."
ISAIAH 26:3 ESV

. . . .

Dear Father, I don't feel peace right now. I feel sadness, darkness, and depression. I feel like I wasn't made for this world, like it's too much for me. Why does life have to hurt so much? But as I look closer at this verse, I'm reminded that when I don't feel peace, it's because I'm focused on the wrong things. I'm looking at the hard things in life instead of at You. I need to keep my eyes, thoughts, and heart on You. I trust You, and I know Your peace is there for the taking. Help me retrain my mind to focus on You. Let me feel Your presence. Conquer this depression that's holding me down, and give me Your peace.

"I have said these things to you, that in me you may have peace. In the world you will have tribulation. But take heart; I have overcome the world."
JOHN 16:33 ESV

. . . .

Dear Father, when You said we'd have troubles in this world, You weren't kidding. Right now, trouble is all I see. I'm just so sad all the time. It feels like a wet, heavy blanket over my spirit. Where is that peace You promised? You said I can have peace *in You.* Help me live *in You,* Lord. I want to crawl up inside Your Spirit, for that's the only safe place I can think of. I feel defeated, but You have overcome the world. Pull me out of this depression, and give me that conquering spirit You spoke of. Help me take heart. Give me courage. And let me feel Your peace.

DISAPPOINTMENT

*" 'For I know the plans that I have for you,'
declares the L*ORD*, 'plans for prosperity and not
for disaster, to give you a future and a hope.' "*
JEREMIAH 29:11 NASB

. . . .

Dear Father, in this verse, You promised Joshua
You had good plans for his future. I know this
promise can be applied to my life as well because
You love me. But when I look at my life, sometimes it feels like a disaster. I wonder if this is
all there is because, if so, it sure seems like a
mess. Can You please give me a glimpse of that
"prosperity" You promised? Can I please have a
little taste of that good future, that good hope
You pledged? Right now I feel disappointed in
my life. But I will trust You. I know Your heart
is for me, and I know You are good.

"Peace I leave you, My peace I give you; not as the world gives, do I give to you. Do not let your hearts be troubled, nor fearful."
JOHN 14:27 NASB

. . . .

Dear Father, right now I feel disappointed in the way things have turned out, and I can't see how things will ever get any better. Yet, I know You are bigger than my worries and fears. I know You are bigger than my circumstances. Help me learn what I can do differently so things will turn out better next time. Use this situation to teach me and make me more like You. I know You have a future planned for me that includes peace and joy and an abundant life that's better than anything I could imagine. I'm clinging to that hope, that promise of a better future. Please let it come soon, Lord.

For I am confident of this very thing, that
He who began a good work among you will
complete it by the day of Christ Jesus.
PHILIPPIANS 1:6 NASB

. . . .

Dear Father, I know You're not finished working in me. I believe that You placed my goals, my dreams, my innermost longings in my heart for a reason and that You want me to live out Your good purpose and plan for my life. But right now, I'm so disappointed. I'm so let down, and I just want to give up. I don't understand Your timeline on things. But I believe, with every disappointment, there's something to learn. Help me learn what I need to so that I can move forward with success. And help me trust Your kindness. If You closed this door, I know You have a better one just around the corner. Give me patience as I trust You for what comes next.

I call upon the LORD, who is worthy to be praised, and I am saved from my enemies.
PSALM 18:3 NASB

. . . .

Dear Father, I've called on You, and I trust You completely. I know this situation isn't over yet, but right now I feel disappointed in the way things have played out. It sure feels like the bad guys are winning. But I know You made me strong, because Your strength lives in me. I know You made me to be a conqueror. I couldn't do that if there weren't something to conquer. If everything came easy, my life story would be pretty dull. Help me hold my chin up and my shoulders back. Give me confidence and a fighting spirit. Help me live out the victory I know You have planned for my life. Most of all, help me trust in Your goodness, Your kindness, and Your love.

From my distress I called upon the Lord; the Lord answered me and put me in an open space. The Lord is for me; I will not fear; what can man do to me? The Lord is for me among those who help me; therefore I will look with satisfaction on those who hate me.
PSALM 118:5–7 NASB

. . . .

Dear Father, I have a lot in common with the person who wrote these verses. I'm distressed, and I'm calling out to You. Please answer me! I feel like everything is crowding in on me, like disappointment is attacking me from every side. Put me in a wide-open space, Father, so I can breathe and be free of this sadness. I know that nothing can compare to Your love and Your salvation. But I want other things too. Help me find favor with people who can help me live out my dreams. Help me find success. When I do, may I use it to honor You.

DISCONTENTMENT

Keep your lives free from the love of money and be content with what you have, because God has said, "Never will I leave you; never will I forsake you."
HEBREWS 13:5 NIV

• •

Dear Father, I don't want to think of myself as materialistic. But the love of money is more than thinking about how much cash I have. This verse is talking about being obsessed with things money can buy. It could even refer to anything other than You. I hate to admit it, but I do think a lot about stuff I'd like to have. I compare my things to other people's things, whether it's their clothes, their houses, their cars, or their toys. But I know *You* are enough. *You* are all I need. Help me redirect my thoughts to You alone. Make me content with what I have because You have blessed me beyond measure.

*Give thanks in all circumstances; for this
is God's will for you in Christ Jesus.*
1 THESSALONIANS 5:18 NIV

. . . .

Dear Father, how am I supposed to give thanks in everything? That doesn't make sense. Some things are pretty rotten, and I'm not thankful for them. But You didn't say I had to be thankful *for* everything. You said I'm supposed to find things to be thankful for in the middle of whatever I'm going through. No matter what happens, You are there. If I look for You, I will find blessings. I'll see Your love, even in the darkest place. Your kindness surrounds me, even when life seems hard and cold. Teach me to have a grateful attitude so I can give thanks in all circumstances. Thank You for choosing me, for loving me, and for making me Your child.

"But seek first his kingdom and his righteousness, and all these things will be given to you as well."
MATTHEW 6:33 NIV

. . . .

Dear Father, You are so generous. You didn't say material things are wrong. It's okay for me to want things. It's just not okay for me to want anything more than I want You. Sometimes, I get a little obsessed about things, and my thoughts focus on whatever I want in the moment. I think about what life would be like if I had nicer clothes or a new car or if I made the team or got the lead in the play or if I were more popular. Those desires aren't wrong. They're just secondary. They won't bring me the joy and peace I want. I can only find true satisfaction in You. Keep my focus on You alone, Lord. I love You above all else.

Take delight in the LORD, and he will give you the desires of your heart.
PSALM 37:4 NIV

. . . .

Dear Father, I can think of a lot of things that make me smile, that bring me temporary joy. But You want to be my main focus, don't You? You want to be the one who brings a smile to my face and joy to my heart. You want to be my first love. You even promise here that if I delight in You, You'll give me the other things my heart desires. When I love You more than anything or anyone, You change my desires to match Your will for me. Thank You for loving me so much that You want to make all my dreams come true. Line up my dreams and desires to match Your best for me. Teach me to delight in You, Lord.

DISTRUST

*And we know that in all things God works
for the good of those who love him, who
have been called according to his purpose.*
ROMANS 8:28 NIV

• •

Dear Father, I know You say all things will work
together for good for those who love You, but
this doesn't feel good. This doesn't feel like
it's going to work out at all. I'm having a hard
time trusting You in this circumstance. Give me
patience, Lord. I want a fast-food, drive-thru
solution. I want everything to work itself out
today. But I know Your timing doesn't work on
my calendar. Even though it's hard to trust You
right now, I will trust You anyway. You are my
only hope. I believe that at some point, sooner
than I might think, I'll be able to look back
on this and see that You were, indeed, working
things out for my good.

*"Do not let your hearts be troubled.
You believe in God; believe also in me."*
JOHN 14:1 NIV

. . . .

Dear Father, I wish I could turn off my emotions as easily as I turn off the lights in my room. You say not to let my heart be troubled, but how can I not be troubled? Am I supposed to push aside all the hard things I face and act like they're not happening? I guess it's a matter of focus. Those emotions will be there, but if I choose to think about my circumstances more than I think about You, I'll crumble. Help me focus on You and Your love for me. Help me believe in Your goodness, Your kindness, and Your love. When troubling thoughts overwhelm me, whisper words of encouragement. I know You have good things in store for me. I choose to hope in You.

Those who know your name trust in you, for you, LORD, have never forsaken those who seek you.
PSALM 9:10 NIV

. . . .

Dear Father, I don't know why I struggle to trust You. When I look back on my life, I see clearly that You've never failed me. You've always been there for me, walking through the fire, carrying me through even the hardest times. You've never forsaken me or left me alone. But the last words of this verse hold an important key: *those who seek You.* Sometimes, I forget to look for You in my troubles. I know if I do, You'll be right there, holding my hand, seeing me through. When I face difficult times, remind me to look for You. Remind me that You're never far away. I love You, I trust You, and I know You won't let me down.

But Jesus would not entrust himself
to them, for he knew all people.
JOHN 2:24 NIV

. . . .

Dear Jesus, when You walked the earth, You knew better than to trust certain people. Somehow, You were able to love them without expecting too much from them. You knew that humans are flawed, and they'll let You down. How can I follow Your example of wisdom plus love? Teach me to have a tender heart toward others and love them without expecting anything in return. Help me know who I can trust and who I need to keep at arm's length. In the past, I've trusted the wrong people, and their failures have made it hard for me to trust anyone. Show me the balance. Surround me with people I can trust, and give me wisdom to know who I can't. Help me love people even when they let me down.

DIVORCE / SEPARATION

*Why are you in despair, my soul? And
why are you restless within me? Wait
for God, for I will again praise Him for
the help of His presence, my God.*
PSALM 42:5 NASB

. . . .

Dear Father, this hurts so much. Two people
I love can't get along. They had to love each
other at some point, or I wouldn't be here.
The idea that their love has failed leaves me
feeling confused, like I'm lost at sea. But I know
there are things going on that I may never fully
understand. Help me love each of my parents
the way You love them. Help me view them with
compassion. Show them how much this hurts
me. Help them get along, even if they can't stay
together. Give me strength to get through this.
Help me breathe. Give me Your peace, Lord.

The steadfast of mind You will keep in
perfect peace, because he trusts in You.
ISAIAH 26:3 NASB

. . . .

Dear Father, to be steadfast means to be dedicated, committed, and unswerving in one's belief. Right now, my whole world seems like it's crashing down, and I don't know what to believe anymore. Everything I thought about my life seems like a lie. But I know, even though my parents' love may have changed and even though they have let me down, You will never change. You will never disappoint me. At the moment, I don't know if I'll ever feel at peace again. But I will trust You, Lord, because You are my only hope. Let me feel Your presence and Your peace. Hold my hand. Carry me through this. I love You, I trust You, and I know that in spite of everything that's happening, You are good.

For His anger is but for a moment, His favor is for a lifetime; weeping may last for the night, but a shout of joy comes in the morning.
PSALM 30:5 NASB

. . . .

Dear Father, in my head, I know You're not angry at me. But in my heart, I feel like You've forgotten me. This hurts so much, and I don't know how I can withstand all this pain. I want my parents to love each other, and the fact that they want to separate makes me question my whole existence. But I trust You that this pain won't last forever. I trust that You'll cause even this to work for my good. I know this experience will make me softer, kinder, and more compassionate to others who are hurting. Help me through this, Lord. If joy comes in the morning, please let morning come soon.

And my God will supply all your needs
according to His riches in glory in Christ Jesus.
PHILIPPIANS 4:19 NASB

. . . .

Dear Father, You promised to supply all my needs. Right now, I don't feel like my needs are being met. I need my parents to get along. I need them to love each other. I need them to stay married and to give me a loving, stable home. But I know, even though I'm hurting right now, You will help me through this. I know You'll be both mother and father to me while my parents are distracted. I know You'll give me the stability and security I long for. Hold me, Father. Whisper Your peace to me. You know everything I'm feeling even better than I do. You're aware of the holes in my spirit right now. Sing to me. Comfort me. Fill in the gaps with Your love.

This is my comfort in my misery,
that Your word has revived me.
PSALM 119:50 NASB

. . . .

Dear Father, I need Your comfort right now. This pain runs deeper than anything I've ever felt. Life feels so unfair. I am truly miserable, but I know You are right here with me. I can feel Your love all around me. You feel every tear, don't You? Thank You for Your Word, because I know there is comfort there. In Your Word, I can find wisdom for how to get through this awful time. Please lead me to the right verses. As I read, speak peace to me. Let me feel Your presence, holding me through the worst of it. Show me how to love my parents. Help me not to take sides, even when I'm tempted. Thank You for holding my hand and loving me through this.

DOUBT

But let him ask in faith, with no doubting,
for the one who doubts is like a wave of the
sea that is driven and tossed by the wind.
JAMES 1:6 ESV

. . . .

Dear Father, I want to have faith. I really do. I want to trust You so much that I'm not anxious or afraid. I know You love me and You'll take care of me. But this world holds some pretty bad stuff, and I don't want to experience those things. Sometimes, life hurts. People disappoint me. Unfortunate things happen, and I'm left wondering how a loving Father would allow such events. And so I doubt. Yet through it all, I know You are kind. Through it all, I know that You are in control and that You're working everything out for my good. Help me set aside my doubt. I want to trust You with all my heart.

*And Jesus answered them, "Truly, I say to you,
if you have faith and do not doubt, you will
not only do what has been done to the fig tree,
but even if you say to this mountain, 'Be taken
up and thrown into the sea,' it will happen."*
MATTHEW 21:21 ESV

. . . .

Dear Father, I have looked at mountains. I've told them to move in Your name, and they've stayed right where they were. I've asked for doors to be opened, sickness to be healed, relationships to be restored. . .and nothing happened. How can I have this kind of faith, when my attempts at faith have failed? Yet, I can also think of times when I cried out to You in the dark and You were there. Times when I didn't think I'd make it through, and You carried me. I guess faith grows over time, with exercise. Grow my faith, Lord. I want to move mountains with You.

And whatever we ask we receive from him, because we keep his commandments and do what pleases him.
1 JOHN 3:22 ESV

. . . .

Dear Father, this verse feels misleading. I've asked for things from You and not received them. I've tried to please You. I've tried to follow Your commandments, but You don't always give me what I want. I guess I need to change my perspective. When I ask for things I need, things that help me live out Your purpose for my life, You always come through. But when I ask selfishly, or when I ask with a warped understanding of what I need, You don't always answer the way I want You to. I know You're a good, kind, loving Father. Sometimes, You withhold things because You know they're not in my best interest. Forgive me for doubting Your love. Help me trust You more.

"Truly, I say to you, whoever says to this mountain, 'Be taken up and thrown into the sea,' and does not doubt in his heart, but believes that what he says will come to pass, it will be done for him."

MARK 11:23 ESV

Dear Father, I know You are God. I know You are all-powerful and almighty. You control the earth on its axis. You place every star in the sky and tell the moon where to stand. I believe You can move mountains. But sometimes when I ask You to move the mountains in my life, I do so with a weak understanding of Your will. I guess faith and trust go together. I ask for what I want, but I trust that Your answer is perfect. Forgive my doubt. Build my faith. I trust You to move the mountains that need to be moved to bring about Your perfect will in my life.

DYSFUNCTIONAL RELATIONSHIPS

One who walks with wise people will be wise,
but a companion of fools will suffer harm.
PROVERBS 13:20 NASB

. . . .

Dear Father, a dysfunctional relationship is one that doesn't function in a healthy way. Instead, it is harmful to the people in the relationship. Some of the relationships in my life are really hard. Instead of building me up, I feel like they're destroying me. I want to surround myself with wise, godly people, but it's hard to get away from the dysfunctional relationships. Help me avoid interacting with toxic people, and give me wisdom and courage to maintain healthy boundaries when I must be around them. Teach me to respond in love and kindness without becoming a doormat for others to walk on. Thank You for teaching me about healthy, loving relationships. Place healthy people in my life, and help me pattern my relationships after those who are doing it right.

*For where jealousy and selfish ambition
exist, there is disorder and every evil thing.*
JAMES 3:16 NASB

. . . .

Dear Father, some of my relationships confuse me. There are people I thought were my friends, but they're competitive, petty, and jealous. They don't celebrate my victories. Instead, they try to make me feel bad about myself. Sometimes, I realize I'm acting the same way toward them. But that's not how You designed relationships to work, is it? Forgive me for falling into that trap. Help me treat others with love and encouragement. And help me disentangle myself from friendships with people who aren't really my friends. Surround me with people who will love, encourage, and support me. Help me treat others that way as well. Teach me to have healthy boundaries with the people around me, and help me correct poor relationship skills in myself. I want to pattern my friendships after the way You love me.

Do not be deceived: "Bad company
corrupts good morals."
1 CORINTHIANS 15:33 NASB

. . . .

Dear Father, more than anything, I want to please You. I want to live in a way that honors You. But when I'm around certain people, it's hard to live for You. Even when I try, I find myself slipping into old habits and ungodly actions. When I'm with them, I find myself gossiping about others, even though I know it's wrong. I find myself lying, cheating, and acting in ways I know are unbecoming of a daughter of the King. Forgive me, Lord. Lead me to a new group of friends. Remind me that my toxic friends are more likely to drag me down to their level than I am to change them. Free me from the ties that connect me to them, and create new bonds with people who will encourage me to live for You.

Do not make friends with a person given to anger, or go with a hot-tempered person, or you will learn his ways and find a snare for yourself.
PROVERBS 22:24–25 NASB

. . . .

Dear Father, sometimes I want to fit in so badly that I'm willing to hang out with whoever will accept me. Those are often people who are negative, who complain about everything, and who are angry at the world. They're willing to accept anyone who will listen to their complaints. But the more I'm around those people, the more I become like them. I don't want to be a negative, unhappy person. I don't want to be angry all the time. I want to be happy and grateful for the life You've given me. Rescue me out of that group, and set me in another, more positive group of friends. I want to surround myself with people who demonstrate Your love, peace, and joy in their lives.

Never repay evil for evil to anyone. Respect what is right in the sight of all people.
ROMANS 12:17 NASB

. . . .

Dear Father, when others are cruel, I want to be cruel back. When others hurt me, I want to hurt them back. An eye for an eye, right? But that's not how You want me to operate. It's hard to accept that I'm supposed to love those who hurt me. I know I'm supposed to leave the revenge to You. If I take things into my own hands and seek revenge, You'll let me, and You'll stay out of it. My anger will destroy me, and it won't make anything better. But if I keep doing my job—to love people—You'll do Your job, which is to enforce justice. Help me treat others with kindness and respect, even when I feel they don't deserve it. I trust You to take care of the justice part.

ENEMIES

"If you listen carefully to what he says and do all that I say, I will be an enemy to your enemies and will oppose those who oppose you."

EXODUS 23:22 NIV

. . . .

Dear Father, in this verse, You sent an angel as a messenger and made this promise to Your people. Instead of an angel, I have Your written Word. I'm listening, Father. I'm trying to obey. But there are mean, cruel people in my life. They want to see me hurt. Please prevent them from succeeding. Make them stop. As hard as my life seems right now, I know You are on my side. And if You are for me, I know my enemies don't have a chance. Remind me to treat them with love and kindness and to trust You to put them in their places. Keep me safe, both physically and emotionally. Thank You for being my defender.

*"But to you who are listening I say: Love
your enemies, do good to those who
hate you, bless those who curse you,
pray for those who mistreat you."*
LUKE 6:27–28 NIV

. . . .

Dear Father, this is a difficult passage. It's a hard
command. How am I supposed to do good to
those who hate me? How can I return cruelty
with love? But that's exactly what You did. When
You walked this earth, You loved the very people
You knew would betray You. I'm not sure I have
that kind of strength. But with You living in me,
I know I don't have to do it on my own. You will
be my power. You'll live out Your love through
me if I'll just be humble, step aside, and let You
work. Make me strong enough to love those
who hate me, Father.

Do not gloat when your enemy falls; when they stumble, do not let your heart rejoice.

. . . .

Dear Father, I don't mean to do it. But secretly, when someone who has mistreated me ends up humiliated or shamed or miserable, something inside me rejoices. I don't want to be vengeful, but it's hard not to feel relief that they're hurting the way they hurt me. In a way, I feel like they deserve what they got. Help me see them the way You see them. Help me understand that when others are cruel, it's often because they've been treated cruelly. Teach me to love my enemies so much that I cry when they cry. I want to live out Your love toward them so they'll see who You are and want to know You. Change my heart. Replace vengeance with compassion, mercy, and love.

*Do not take revenge, my dear friends,
but leave room for God's wrath, for it is
written: "It is mine to avenge; I will repay,"
says the Lord. On the contrary: "If your
enemy is hungry, feed him; if he is thirsty,
give him something to drink. In doing this,
you will heap burning coals on his head."*
ROMANS 12:19–20 NIV

Dear Father, when I focus on revenge, I end up bitter. I know bitterness will destroy me. I know I can leave the vengeance to You. You'll take care of things much better than I can. Help me lay all my hurt, anger, and bad memories at Your feet. Help me breathe out those bad thoughts and breathe in Your love. Take all the negative feelings and replace them with Your grace. Help me love those who have hurt me, because love—not hate—will change me into the kind of person I want to be.

FACING DEATH

*Jesus said to her, "I am the resurrection
and the life. Whoever believes in me,
though he die, yet shall he live, and
everyone who lives and believes in me
shall never die. Do you believe this?"*
JOHN 11:25–26 ESV

· ·

Dear Father, I believe in eternal life. I believe
that with You, we'll live forever. But right now,
I'm dealing with separation from someone I
love. I don't want to do life without this person.
I don't want us to be separated. As I face being
apart from my loved one for a long time, I'll need
Your help. I'll need courage, because life without
this person will seem scary. I'll need strength,
because there will be days when I won't want to
go on. But I know Your love brings healing. And
I know this separation is just a "See you later."
One day, we'll be together again, and that time,
the reunion will be permanent.

So is it with the resurrection of the dead. What is sown is perishable; what is raised is imperishable. It is sown in dishonor; it is raised in glory. It is sown in weakness; it is raised in power. It is sown a natural body; it is raised a spiritual body. If there is a natural body, there is also a spiritual body.
1 Corinthians 15:42–44 esv

· ·

Dear Father, I know there are some things I'll never fully understand while I'm on this earth. Death is one of them. The only life I understand right now is this current one I live in my physical body. When my loved one dies, I'll miss their physical presence. Help me understand things that are above me. Help me know, deep in my spirit, that death is just a temporary separation and that one day I'll be reunited with You and with all those I loved who chose You in this life.

For this light momentary affliction is preparing for us an eternal weight of glory beyond all comparison, as we look not to the things that are seen but to the things that are unseen. For the things that are seen are transient, but the things that are unseen are eternal.
2 CORINTHIANS 4:17–18 ESV

. . . .

Dear Father, right now, this real, physical life is the only reality I know. All the spiritual stuff seems like a nice idea, but it doesn't feel real. But according to this verse, heaven is more "real" than the life I'm living now, because heaven is eternal. Help me understand that this life was never meant to be permanent. This life is just a preparation for better things to come. As I say a temporary goodbye to people I love, remind me that one day I'll celebrate with You—and them—for eternity. And it will be more real than anything I've ever known.

*Yes, we are of good courage, and
we would rather be away from the
body and at home with the Lord.*
2 CORINTHIANS 5:8 ESV

. . . .

Dear Father, I know heaven holds amazing things for those who love You. I know that after experiencing Your presence, no one would choose to be back here. But I'm selfish. I don't want to be separated from the people I love. I know heaven is a better place, but I don't want the person I love to be in a better place. I want that person here, with me. I want to share my present, physical life with the people who are important to me, and death prevents that. Help me understand. Help me rejoice for my loved one. Heal my pain and comfort my sorrow as I learn to do life, and even to experience joy, without them.

*"He will wipe away every tear from their eyes,
and death shall be no more, neither shall there
be mourning, nor crying, nor pain anymore,
for the former things have passed away."*

REVELATION 21:4 ESV

. . . .

Dear Father, I love this promise that one day I won't be sad anymore. One day, when I get to heaven, I'll never feel sorrow again. But right now, I'm devastated. Right now, I don't know how I'll make it through life without my loved one. This person was such an important part of who I am, and now, everything has changed. The air feels different. Everything I do feels like I'm doing it under water, like I can't breathe or walk the same without my person here on this earth. It's hard to see others going on with their lives when I'm in such pain. Comfort me now, Lord. I need Your strength, Your compassion, and Your peace.

FAILURE

"You shall say to them, Thus says the LORD:
When men fall, do they not rise again?
If one turns away, does he not return?"
JEREMIAH 8:4 RSV

. . . .

Dear Father, I know when I fall, You'll pick me up. You've given me strength and courage to learn from my mistakes and do better next time. But right now, this failure hurts. Right now, it feels like all I do is fail, and I'm ready to give up. I know You care about my failures. I can feel You with me right now, encouraging me, telling me that I'm strong. Help me learn from my mistakes. And keep reminding me that You love me because of *who I am*, not because of *what I do*. You love me in spite of my mess-ups. Help me through this hard season, and give me wisdom and courage to do better next time.

*For a righteous man falls seven
times, and rises again; but the wicked
are overthrown by calamity.*
PROVERBS 24:16 RSV

. . . .

Dear Father, sometimes I equate failure with not being good enough. But according to this verse, the righteous fail sometimes. I can be Your child and still fall down. But as Your child, I'll get back up. As Your child, I'm not defined by my mistakes or shortcomings. Instead, each failure is simply an opportunity to learn, grow, and become more of the person You created me to be. A winner isn't the person who never falls—it's the person who keeps getting up, keeps moving forward in spite of failure. Thank You for this reminder that I'm Your child. I'm more than a conqueror. I will not give up. With Your strength, I will learn, grow, and become more like You.

We are afflicted in every way, but not crushed; perplexed, but not driven to despair; persecuted, but not forsaken; struck down, but not destroyed.
2 CORINTHIANS 4:8–9 RSV

. . . .

Dear Father, I tried my best, but my best wasn't good enough. It seems that no matter how hard I try, I'm always the runner-up. I'm never the winner. I know You want me to be humble, because humility is a godly trait. But it would be nice if, just once, I could succeed. It would be nice if, just once, I could be first place. I know You love me. You know all my hopes, dreams, and desires, and You want to bless me. Line up my goals with Your plans for my life. Help me be truly happy for the people who always seem to win. I trust that one day, in Your perfect timing, I'll have my moment to shine. Until then, I'll trust You.

He drew me up from the desolate pit, out of the miry bog, and set my feet upon a rock, making my steps secure. He put a new song in my mouth, a song of praise to our God. Many will see and fear, and put their trust in the LORD.
PSALM 40:2–3 RSV

. . . .

Dear Father, this verse says You'll lift me out of the pit and set me on a high place. I feel like I'm in the pit right now. No matter how hard I try, it seems like I always end up back at the bottom, covered in mud and slime. But I refuse to stay there. No matter how many times I slip and fall, I'll keep reaching for You. I'll hold up my arms knowing You'll lift me up, clean me off, and give me a new start. Thank You for that kind of confidence. I'll keep trying, Lord.

The steps of a man are from the LORD, and he establishes him in whose way he delights; though he fall, he shall not be cast headlong, for the LORD is the stay of his hand.
PSALM 37:23–24 RSV

. . . .

Dear Father, sometimes I think that following You means I won't mess up. But obviously, that's not true. I try to obey You. I try to please You. But here I am, once again, in the middle of a mess I made myself. Forgive me. I know You love me, and even this won't keep me from living out Your purpose for my life. Even when I blow it, You've got me. You're right there, ready to lift me up, ready to coach me and encourage me and set me back on the right path. Thank You for holding on to me even when I fail. I love You, and I trust that Your plans for me are good.

FAMILY STRESS

Put on a heart of compassion, kindness,
humility, gentleness, and patience; bearing
with one another, and forgiving each other,
whoever has a complaint against anyone; just
as the Lord forgave you, so must you do also.
COLOSSIANS 3:12–13 NASB

. . . .

Dear Father, sometimes it's really hard living in my family. I look at other people's families, and they seem a lot happier than we are. I wish my family were normal. Or different. But this is the family You've given me, so I'm asking for Your help. Help me love them the way You want me to love them. I can't change them—only You can do that. So please change me from the inside out. Give me the traits that will make it easier to live with the people in my family. Give me compassion, kindness, humility, gentleness, and patience. Help me love and forgive. Make me like You.

Children, obey your parents in the Lord, for this is right. Honor your father and mother (which is the first commandment with a promise), so that it may turn out well for you, and that you may live long on the earth.

EPHESIANS 6:1–3 NASB

. . . .

Dear Father, I know I'm supposed to obey my parents. But they treat me like I'm a little child. It's hard to obey them when I think they're wrong. But I'm still dependent on them for many things. They pay for stuff I need. They drive me places when I need a ride. And they provide me a place to live and sleep and shower; I know I should respect them for those and so many other reasons. Help me do the hard things, Lord. Help me obey my parents, even when I don't agree with them. I know my obedience will remove a lot of stress from our family.

*Listen, my son, to your father's instruction,
and do not ignore your mother's teaching.*
PROVERBS 1:8 NASB

. . . .

Dear Father, it's hard to listen to my parents when they don't listen to me. It's hard to respect them when they don't respect me. But I know that, even if they don't understand what's going on in my head, they do love me. They do want what's best for me, even if they don't see things the way I do. Help me listen to them. Remind me that they've been through more stuff than I have, and they do have wisdom that I don't have. Help me trust their love for me, even when I don't like what they say. Most of all, help me trust *Your* love for me. I want to please You, and I know listening to my parents is what You want me to do.

For I consider that the sufferings of this present time are not worthy to be compared with the glory that is to be revealed to us.
ROMANS 8:18 NASB

. . . .

Dear Father, I know I shouldn't feel this way, but sometimes I can't stand living in this family. Nobody gets along. Everybody's stressed out, and it never seems to get better. I just want to go live somewhere else. . .someplace where there is love and laughter and kindness. But this is where You've placed me, Lord. Instead of wanting to escape, maybe I should think of ways to make this home the kind of place I want it to be. Make me more loving. Make me kind. Show me how to make the people in my family smile. Shine through me, and work a miracle in our home. Remove the stress and replace it with Your peace.

Do not speak against one another, brothers and sisters. The one who speaks against a brother or sister, or judges his brother or sister, speaks against the law and judges the law; but if you judge the law, you are not a doer of the law but a judge of it.
JAMES 4:11 NASB

. . . .

Dear Father, I get so frustrated with my family. It's hard not to complain about them to my friends or even on social media. When I tell people how awful they are, I get some sympathy and understanding. But I know when I complain to others about my family, it only causes more stress. They get their feelings hurt, and I hang on to my anger and frustration. Give me wisdom to know when to share private things and who to share them with. Help me keep petty complaints between You and me. Teach me to love my family the way I want them to love me.

FEELING DIFFERENT

His disciples asked him, "Rabbi, who sinned, this man or his parents, that he was born blind?" "Neither this man nor his parents sinned," said Jesus, "but this happened so that the works of God might be displayed in him. As long as it is day, we must do the works of him who sent me. Night is coming, when no one can work."
JOHN 9:2–4 NIV

. . . .

Dear Father, I have a really hard time understanding why I was born the way I was. Why can't I just be normal? Why do I have to struggle with things that most people don't struggle with? It doesn't seem fair. If what this verse says is true, that You allow certain things so Your presence can be displayed in people's lives, then I want You to show off in my life. Whatever abilities I have or don't have. . .they're all Yours. When others see me, let them see You.

Moses said to the LORD, "Pardon your servant, Lord. I have never been eloquent, neither in the past nor since you have spoken to your servant. I am slow of speech and tongue." The LORD said to him, "Who gave human beings their mouths? Who makes them deaf or mute? Who gives them sight or makes them blind? Is it not I, the LORD? Now go; I will help you speak and will teach you what to say."

EXODUS 4:10–12 NIV

. . . .

Dear Father, like Moses, I struggle with abilities. It's hard for me to do things that are easy for other people. Yet, I know You made me this way for a specific purpose, even if I don't understand it. I trust You to help me achieve the things I need to accomplish. Help me, Lord, and fill in the gaps. In my weakness, be my strength.

You knit me together in my mother's womb. I praise you because I am fearfully and wonderfully made; your works are wonderful, I know that full well.
PSALM 139:13–14 NIV

. . . .

Dear Father, when I compare myself to others, I don't always feel "fearfully and wonderfully made." I feel like You messed up, like somebody spilled coffee on the blueprint of my life. Yet, I know that's not true. I know You don't make mistakes. And I know that in all the world, there is no one else exactly like me. I can reflect Your love and Your character in a way that no one else can. Surround me with people who need what I have to give. Make me a mirror of You so everyone can know Your goodness, kindness, and compassion. Shine through me, Father. When others look at me, don't let them see my differences. Let them only see Your love.

"For My thoughts are not your thoughts,
nor are your ways My ways," declares the
LORD. *"For as the heavens are higher than*
the earth, so are My ways higher than your
ways and my thoughts than your thoughts."
ISAIAH 55:8–9 NASB

· ·

Dear Father, I don't understand why You made me the way I am. Sometimes, it feels pointless and doesn't make any sense. I look at others who seem to have everything so easy, and my life seems unfair. Yet, I know everyone struggles. Their problems just may not be as visible as mine. Help me understand, Father. And when I don't understand, help me trust in Your goodness, Your kindness, and Your love. I know You made me with a unique plan and purpose. I know my differentness isn't a mistake; it's an opportunity to share Your love in a unique way. Help me live out Your purpose for my life. When others look at me, let them see a reflection of You.

FINANCIAL STRESS

And my God will meet all your needs according to the riches of his glory in Christ Jesus.
PHILIPPIANS 4:19 NIV

· ·

Dear Father, I hate it when my parents fight about money. I hate it when I'm afraid to ask for the things I need because I don't want to cause more stress. It really stinks, not knowing if there will be enough. And it's awful when my friends have nicer things than I do and I feel like I'm not as good as they are because of it. More money would solve so many problems. But I know money can't bring happiness. You alone are the source of true joy and peace. Help me trust You, knowing You'll supply all my needs. Please send what we need so my family doesn't have to be so stressed. I trust in Your goodness, Your kindness, and Your generosity.

"But blessed is the one who trusts in the LORD, whose confidence is in him. They will be like a tree planted by the water that sends out its roots by the stream. It does not fear when heat comes; its leaves are always green. It has no worries in a year of drought and never fails to bear fruit."
JEREMIAH 17:7–8 NIV

. . . .

Dear Father, as I read through that passage, I feel like my family is in a "year of drought." I worry that we won't have enough money for the things we need. But I'm learning the difference between my wants and my needs. The truth is, many of the things I want don't end up bringing me as much joy as I thought they would. What I need is Your love. I need security. I need friends and family and a safe place to live. Thank You for giving me everything I need.

But remember the LORD your God, for it is he who gives you the ability to produce wealth, and so confirms his covenant, which he swore to your ancestors, as it is today.
DEUTERONOMY 8:18 NIV

· ·

Dear Father, You give us the ability to produce wealth, but You don't want us to focus on money. Instead, You want our main focus to be on You. What abilities have You given me, Lord? What talents and skills can I develop so I can have what I need and provide for my family one day? Help me honor You with all I have. Give me the chance to be educated, and help me take advantage of opportunities to learn what I can so I can take care of myself, help others, and be generous with those who are going through hardship. Thank You for providing everything I need.

The Lord will grant you abundant prosperity—
in the fruit of your womb, the young of your
livestock and the crops of your ground—in the
land he swore to your ancestors to give you.
DEUTERONOMY 28:11 NIV

. . . .

Dear Father, You promised prosperity for Your children. Right now, I don't feel prosperous. Prosperity goes beyond basic needs and means you have a lot of what you want as well. But my definition of prosperity is different from Yours, isn't it? You do give me what I need, and I'm so grateful for it. But You've given me so much more, and those blessings don't have anything to do with a bank account. You've given me people to love. You've given me the sunrise and sunset. You've given me music and colors and imagination. You've given me Your Son, and You've given me peace. Thank You for the prosperity You've poured out on my life.

FRENEMIES / TOXIC FRIENDSHIPS

If someone says, "I love God," and yet
he hates his brother or sister, he is a liar;
for the one who does not love his brother
and sister whom he has seen, cannot
love God, whom he has not seen.
1 JOHN 4:20 NASB

. . . .

Dear Father, I have friends who make me feel horrible about myself. When John wrote about hate here, he wasn't talking about a wish-you-were-dead feeling. Rather, he was writing in extremes, to make a point. According to Your Word, love is patient, kind, and encouraging. It's not jealous or easily offended. Love builds up; it doesn't tear down. Love protects; it doesn't purposely cause pain. Help me recognize the difference between a friend and a "frenemy." Surround me with true friends, and help me avoid the people who don't love me like You love. Finally, help me to be a true friend to others, and keep me from hurting others the way they have hurt me.

A friend loves at all times, and a
brother is born for adversity.
PROVERBS 17:17 NASB

. . . .

Dear Father, I have friends who are hot and cold. They may "love" me sometimes, but it's not a persistent, loyal kind of love. They're good to me while I'm useful, but they drop me when someone better comes along. They say things that make me feel bad and make me question my worth. Help me learn from what I feel right now. I don't want to ever treat anyone the way I've been treated. Help me model true love and friendship. Teach me healthy boundaries and how to respectfully cut those people from my life who don't build me up and encourage me to be all You created me to be. I'm lonely, and I need friends. Send me true friends who will really care about me for the long haul.

And when he comes to see me, he speaks
empty words; his heart gathers wickedness
to itself; when he goes outside, he tells it.
PSALM 41:6 NASB

. . . .

Dear Father, some people say nice things to my face, but they say unkind things about me to others. Give me wisdom to know who to trust and who to hold at arm's length. Give me courage to stand firm, even when untrustworthy people try to draw me in. Most of all, teach me to be consistent in my character. Help me to be kind, encouraging, and respectful to others, both to their faces and behind their backs. When I'm around people who want to gossip and slander others, remind me of how much gossip hurts. Make me brave enough to say something kind about the person who is being talked about. Then help me leave the conversation. Give me friends who will do the same for me.

Even my close friend in whom I trusted, who ate my bread, has lifted up his heel against me.
PSALM 41:9 NASB

. . . .

Dear Jesus, betrayal hurts deeply. You know about betrayal, don't You? Judas was one of Your closest friends. You invited him into Your inner circle and shared Your true self with him. Still, in the end, he turned against You for a few silver coins. Some of my friends turned against me for popularity or for other reasons. I know that even when people let me down, You never will. You are always for me. You are always working things out for my good. I need in-the-flesh, human friends too. Please send authentic friends into my life, and help me recognize them when they show up. Most of all, help me never hurt someone the way I've been hurt. Make me the kind of friend I want others to be to me.

The LORD said to Eliphaz the Temanite, "My wrath is kindled against you and against your two friends, because you have not spoken of Me what is trustworthy, as My servant Job has."
JOB 42:7 NASB

. . . .

Dear Father, when Job suffered, his friends told him it was his fault. Instead of supporting and encouraging him, they told him he must have done something to deserve it. Job didn't even have to respond. You stepped in and put them in their places. Will You do the same for me? My friend has disappointed and hurt me deeply. Like Job's friends, she has accused me of things that aren't true. Will You convict her heart and show her the truth? Will You be my defender in this situation? I am powerless to change what others think, but You control all things. I trust You to handle this. Thank You for loving me and taking care of my problems.

GOING THROUGH CHANGE

*The Lord is my rock and my fortress
and my deliverer, my God, my rock, in
whom I take refuge, my shield, and the
horn of my salvation, my stronghold.*
PSALM 18:2 ESV

. . . .

Dear Father, I don't like change. It's uncomfortable. I wish everything could stay the same. But I know change is a necessary part of life. Sometimes, the change feels good, but most of the time, it feels awkward and scary. I know that no matter what changes I face, You will stay the same. If I move to a new school or neighborhood or even out of state, You are there. If things in my family change, You are constant. Friends may come and go, but You will never leave me or forsake me. Thank You for being my rock. When change threatens my peace, I'll trust You, and I know I'll find rest.

*Every good gift and every perfect gift
is from above, coming down from the
Father of lights, with whom there is no
variation or shadow due to change.*
JAMES 1:17 ESV

. . . .

Dear Father, You are full of wonderful surprises, aren't You? You always have good gifts and sweet blessings in store for those who love You. But change is sometimes necessary in order for those good gifts to show up. Change is hard for me. It's easier to stay with what's comfortable, even if I know it's not best. Help me embrace the good changes You have for me. Help me walk through the doors You open, even when I don't know what's on the other side. In the middle of change, I know Your love, Your kindness, and Your goodness are constant. *Change* is just another word for transformation. I know You're transforming me into the person You created me to be.

*Jesus Christ is the same yesterday
and today and forever.*
HEBREWS 13:8 ESV

. . . .

Dear Jesus, thank You for being constant. Thank You for staying the same. When everything in this world is in chaos, You are steady. When everything is changing, You don't move. Right now, my world seems crazy and scary, like it's spinning out of control, and I need something solid to cling to. You are that something. In the middle of the storm, I'll hold on to You. Even better, I know You're holding on to me. Even if I let go, even if circumstances pull at me, keep me close. Keep me safe. When the world howls, whisper peace into my spirit. I know that You love me and You'll never let me go. Thank You for that assurance and for the confidence I have in Your love, no matter what.

"Be strong and courageous. Do not fear or be in dread of them, for it is the Lord your God who goes with you. He will not leave you or forsake you."
DEUTERONOMY 31:6 ESV

. . . .

Dear Father, I'm facing some big changes in my life, and I'm afraid. I know all the right things to say and think. I know I'm supposed to be confident and strong. But deep down, I feel like a little child at her first day of preschool who just wants her mommy. The good news is I know You won't drop me off at this new circumstance and leave me there. You will go with me. You'll hold my hand and stay by my side through each new encounter. Thank You for the promise never to leave me or forsake me. I'll hold tight to Your hand, and I'll trust in Your goodness. Thank You for giving me courage and strength to face new things.

*For everything there is a season, and a
time for every matter under heaven.*
ECCLESIASTES 3:1 ESV

. . . .

Dear Father, You designed this life for change, didn't You? Some change can be exciting, like when spring turns into summer with long, lazy days at the pool and hours to do whatever I want. Other times, it means changing my routine and meeting new people and adjusting to new circumstances. Some change involves saying goodbye to people and places I love, and that hurts. But each season has its own beauty. One season must end for the new one to come with all its blessings and adventures. Just as sunny, summer days give way to bright fall colors, one chapter of my life must close in order to open up new chances for growth. Give me strength and confidence to embrace change. Walk with me into this new season. I trust that You have good things in store for me there.

GRIEF

*"So you have sorrow now, but I will see
you again and your hearts will rejoice,
and no one will take your joy from you."*
JOHN 16:22 RSV

. . . .

Dear Father, right now, I'm so filled with grief I can't imagine ever feeling better. I just want to cry or sleep all the time. There's a constant ache in my chest. I never knew sadness could be such a physical sensation. I need to feel this. I need to go through the grieving process. But I don't want to stay here. Teach me how to take small, healthy steps to get through this dark tunnel to the light at the other end. Remind me to do the little things in my control, like eating healthy foods, listening to uplifting music, and spending time each day being grateful for the good things You've blessed me with. I know joy will come back eventually. Thank You for walking with me on this journey.

My flesh and my heart may fail, but God is the strength of my heart and my portion for ever.
PSALM 73:26 RSV

. . . .

Dear Father, I don't know how my heart keeps beating. Right now, it feels like it will cave in on itself. *Sad* isn't a strong enough word for what I feel. It's more like I'm drowning, but there's plenty of air. The air just doesn't fill up my lungs like it used to. God, I need You to be my strength right now. I need You to carry me through this dark time. I know You love me. You promised to never leave me. And You promised joy and peace and blessing for those who follow You. Hold me, Father. Wrap Your arms around me so I can feel Your presence. I trust in Your goodness and love to see me through. I know better days are ahead.

He heals the brokenhearted,
and binds up their wounds.
PSALM 147:3 RSV

• •

Dear Father, why do we have to have our hearts broken? Why do we have to be sad? Why is that a part of human experience? I know we live in a fallen, broken world. I know people sin, disease exists, and bad things happen. But I also know You love me. I need to feel Your presence right now. You promised to heal broken hearts. Here I am. . .my heart is in pieces. I know You will put it back together, better than before. Thank You for being my healer, my comforter, and my friend. I'll hold on to You, trust in Your goodness, and keep breathing. I know one day I'll look back on this and tell others about the miracle You worked in the middle of my grief.

"Come to me, all who labor and are heavy laden, and I will give you rest."
MATTHEW 11:28 RSV

. . . .

Dear Father, I lie down at night, but I can't sleep. I only cry. Several times a night, I have to turn my pillow to the dry side. I can't function. My heart is too heavy for me. In this verse, You invite people like me to come to You. Here I am, Lord. I'm a mess. I don't have strength to go on. Will You be my strength? I can't sleep. Will You calm my thoughts and help me rest? Outside of You, I have no hope. But with You, I know hope is certain. I trust Your goodness, Your kindness, and Your love. I know one day, somehow, You'll bring me through this to a better tomorrow. I don't understand what I'm going through. I don't like it at all. But I will trust You.

GUILT

*For God did not send his Son into
the world to condemn the world,
but to save the world through him.*
JOHN 3:17 NIV

• •

Dear Father, I've messed up. Again. And I feel horrible. When I made the choice to do what I did, I didn't think through the consequences. Now I've hurt people, and my insides feel like a big pile of tangled knots. I want to move forward and make things right, but all I can think about is how stupid my choices were, and I feel frozen in that place. Yet, You knew we'd make bad decisions before You ever created us. You knew we'd goof up, time and again. Thank You for this reminder that it's not Your goal to condemn me and make me feel worse about myself. You want to set me free so I can move forward with a clean slate. Thank You for forgiveness and for fresh starts.

*If we confess our sins, he is faithful
and just and will forgive us our sins and
purify us from all unrighteousness.*
1 JOHN 1:9 NIV

Dear Father, I'm happy to confess my sins. But there are so many to confess. I've dug myself so deeply into a hole of regret that I don't know if I'll ever find my way out. But here I am, at the bottom, Lord. I'm so sorry for all the mistakes I've made. I'm sorry for not listening to You and not listening to the people who love me. I'm sorry for hurting You and others. Thank You for forgiving me. Thank You for not holding my past failures against me. Show me how to make things right with the people I've hurt. Help me move forward with wisdom, confidence, and love. I don't want to repeat the same mistakes.

As far as the east is from the west, so far has he removed our transgressions from us.
PSALM 103:12 NIV

. . . .

Dear Father, You have an ability that humans don't have. You can choose to remove things from Your memory. It's not that You don't remember. . .You just choose to forget. When You forgive me for something, my slate is wiped clean. As far as You're concerned, it's gone. My mind doesn't work that way. As soon as I think I've moved on from my mistakes, Satan whispers in my ear. He reminds me of how badly I've messed up. It's hard not to listen to him, and at that point, I want to give up. When that happens, remind me that Satan is a liar. Remind me that all my sins, faults, and failures have been paid in full and erased from my record. Thank You for loving me enough to remove my guilt from me.

Therefore if anyone is in Christ, this person is a new creation; the old things passed away; behold, new things have come.
2 CORINTHIANS 5:17 NASB

. . . .

Dear Father, this verse always reminds me of a butterfly emerging fresh and new from its chrysalis. It's gone from a plain-Jane caterpillar, crawling on the ground and eating people's garden vegetables, to a beautiful, unique creature of beauty. I feel stuck in the caterpillar stage, Lord, and everything I do seems wrong. I've done so many things I regret, so many things I wish I could go back and do over. But here I am, admitting all this to You, asking You to forgive me and give me a fresh start. I know those wings may not emerge overnight. But through time, as I follow You, I know You'll change me. Help me forget the person I was and trust that You're making me into something new, beautiful, and Christlike.

HEALTH ISSUES

Fear not, for I am with you; be not dismayed, for I am your God; I will strengthen you, I will help you, I will uphold you with my righteous right hand.
ISAIAH 41:10 ESV

. . . .

Dear Father, I don't understand why some people get to be healthy and strong, while others struggle with basic tasks. I don't know why some people's bodies work the way they're supposed to and others don't. It doesn't seem fair, and the people around me who don't struggle like I do really don't understand what it's like. I feel isolated and alone. But even though I don't understand Your purpose, I trust Your goodness. I know You don't make mistakes. And I know You'll use this situation to help me share Your love in a unique way. Thank You for making me strong and for staying with me in the process.

"Behold, I will bring to it health and healing, and I will heal them and reveal to them abundance of prosperity and security."
JEREMIAH 33:6 ESV

. . . .

Dear Father, in this verse, You're talking about healing the nation of Israel after calamity and destruction. I'd really like this verse to be about me. I want to read that You'll bring me health and healing, prosperity and security. I know You love me and want good things for my life. I know You created me for a purpose, and as long as I seek You and follow You, You'll make sure that purpose is completed. And I know that one day, when I stand before You in heaven, I'll be completely healed. I'd like You to heal me on earth. That's my request, Lord. But regardless of what You choose to do in my life, I will trust Your love for me.

*Jesus answered, "It was not that this man
sinned, or his parents, but that the works
of God might be displayed in him."*
JOHN 9:3 ESV

. . . .

Dear Father, in this passage, when people asked whose fault it was that a man was born blind, Jesus put them in their places. He told them it was nobody's fault. Instead, the man's blindness offered a chance for You to show off. Then Jesus healed the man. For the first time in his life, that man could see! Father, I want You to heal me like You healed that man. I'd like to be healthy and strong, like other people I know. But most of all, I want You to show off in my life. Give me strength to endure whatever comes. When others see me, let them see Your goodness, Your kindness, and Your love.

*Now may the Lord of peace himself
give you peace at all times in every
way. The Lord be with you all.*
2 Thessalonians 3:16 esv

. . . .

Dear Father, I don't understand why some people get to be healthy and others have to struggle with sickness and disease. When I think about illness, I don't feel peace. But this verse says You give us peace *at all times in every way.* I guess this is an opportunity for me to experience Your peace and Your presence in my life. I want healing, Lord. That's what I'm asking for, what I'm trusting You for. But I know many people who are healthy physically, but their spirits are sick. I guess they need healing more than someone who is physically ill but at peace. Give me Your peace, Father. Make my spirit strong and whole and healthy. Let me shine Your love to the people who need it.

INSOMNIA

In peace I will both lie down and sleep, for You alone, LORD, have me dwell in safety.
PSALM 4:8 NASB

. . . .

Dear Father, I wish I could sleep. No matter how tired I am, as soon as I lie down, my brain switches into high gear. Everything that bothers me—all my fear and anxiety—swoops in and commands my attention. At night, everything seems worse than it is in the daytime when I'm rested. At night, my thoughts convince me that the worst will happen and nothing will work out for my good. Help me recognize those thoughts as lies. Calm my spirit, soothe my worries, and help me sleep peacefully. I know You have everything under control, and You're working it all out for my good. I'm exhausted, and I know sleep will help me face everything with more confidence. Give me peace and help me sleep.

When you lie down, you will not be afraid;
when you lie down, your sleep will be sweet.
PROVERBS 3:24 NASB

. . . .

Dear Father, I claim this promise right now. I don't know why I can't sleep. Every time I try, negative thoughts show up and command center stage in my mind. It's like they've been hiding in the background, waiting for me to be tired and vulnerable, and then they pounce. Fight those thoughts, Lord. Push them aside. Fill my mind with thoughts of Your love. Whisper a lullaby of Your peace, and remind me that You're right here with me. Push out the negative thoughts with Your truths: You love me, You have good things in store for me, You'll never leave me, and You're always on my side. Help me memorize scriptures to substitute for the fears. When lies threaten to steal my rest, feed me the truth of Your Word until I fall asleep.

I was crying out to the LORD with my voice, and He answered me from His holy mountain. Selah. I lay down and slept; I awoke, for the LORD sustains me.
PSALM 3:4–5 NASB

· ·

Dear Father, when David wrote this, he was on the run from his own son who was trying to overthrow him as king. He didn't run because he was afraid. He ran because he didn't want to face his son in a battle no one would win. David's heart was broken. I can only imagine how hard it was for him to sleep. Yet, he cried out to You, and You calmed his spirit. You helped him rest, and You woke him up the next morning. Do the same for me. You know all my thoughts and fears. Calm my spirit and help me sleep. I know You'll wake me up in the morning refreshed, ready to face a new day.

*Until now you have asked for nothing
in My name; ask and you will receive,
so that your joy may be made full.*
JOHN 16:24 NASB

. . . .

Dear Father, I know this verse doesn't mean You'll supply a never-ending Christmas list. You don't honor selfish requests. But You did promise to meet all my needs, and I need sleep. I'm so tired, Lord, but sleep won't come. I'm asking You—begging You—calm my spirit. Make my thoughts be still so I can rest. Give me strength and self-discipline to push aside those anxious thoughts. Help me tell them to get lost as I focus on Your goodness, Your kindness, and Your love. I want to fall asleep in Your arms, whispering my prayers. Let me feel Your presence and Your peace as I drift into sweet dreams of Your everlasting love.

JEALOUSY

*Love is patient and kind; love does not
envy or boast; it is not arrogant.*
1 CORINTHIANS 13:4 ESV

. . . .

Dear Father, in my head, I know what love should look like. Jealousy is not a characteristic of love. But in my heart, I struggle with comparison. I look at others' lives, and they seem to have so much more than I do. Compared to people I know, I feel less attractive, less successful, less talented. I feel like I'm not as smart, like they have all the breaks and I don't. I don't want to feel that way, but the thoughts and comparisons fill my mind. Help me realize that I only see the good parts of others' lives. Teach me to see myself the way You see me and to be grateful for all the ways You've blessed me. Teach me to be content with my own life and truly happy for others' blessings.

A tranquil heart gives life to the flesh,
but envy makes the bones rot.
PROVERBS 14:30 ESV

. . . .

Dear Father, it's hard not to be jealous of others when everything seems to come so easily for them. Why do some people get to be pretty, smart, and have great families? My life just doesn't seem to measure up. Deep down, I know Satan uses others' blessings to try and make me feel bad about myself. He's a liar and a sneak. I may never know the difficulties other people face. But I do know You love me. I need to stop focusing on everyone else and look to You. You have been so good to me. You have given me people to love. You've given me unique skills and talents. You've placed me at this time and location, in this specific body, in this specific family to help me live out Your purpose for my life. Thank You for loving me so much.

Wrath is cruel, anger is overwhelming,
but who can stand before jealousy?
PROVERBS 27:4 ESV

. . . .

Dear Father, jealousy is such a nasty disease. It gets in my skin, seeps into my heart, and fills every part of me with a sick, nauseous kind of anger. And it's pointless! You love all Your children, and You bless each one in unique ways. There's no use comparing my life to anyone else's. Someone else may not have my problems, but they also don't have my blessings. I need Your help, Father. I don't want to feel this way anymore. I want to be truly happy for the good things in others' lives. I want to be overwhelmed with Your goodness to me instead of angry at what I don't have. Heal me of this disease, and replace it with gratitude and contentment.

You desire and do not have, so you murder.
You covet and cannot obtain, so you fight and
quarrel. You do not have, because you do not
ask. You ask and do not receive, because you
ask wrongly, to spend it on your passions.
JAMES 4:2–3 ESV

. . . .

Dear Father, I may not have murdered anyone because of jealousy, but I haven't had kind thoughts toward them either. I get annoyed with them, even though they haven't done anything wrong. When I focus on what others have that I want, I forget to focus on all the great things You've given me. When I pour my thoughts and attention on anyone other than You, I lose—every time. Teach me to push aside those jealous feelings. Help me be truly happy for others, the way I want them to be when good things happen to me. Most of all, help me focus on all the ways You've poured out Your love to me.

Do nothing from selfish ambition or conceit, but in humility count others more significant than yourselves.
PHILIPPIANS 2:3 ESV

. . . .

Dear Father, humility is a hard concept. When I'm jealous of others, I'm really showing a lack of humility. In my mind, I think I'm more deserving of their blessings than they are. That kind of attitude is insulting to the other person, and it's insulting to You. I know You bless each person according to the unique plans You have for her life. I've heard that if we don't humble ourselves, life will humble us, and that's never fun. I want to humble myself. Teach me to be happy for others and content with my own life. Help me treat others like they're more deserving than I am, and like it's an honor for me to be in their presence. That's humility. That's how You treated others. Make me like You.

LONELINESS

What, then, shall we say in response to these things? If God is for us, who can be against us?
ROMANS 8:31 NIV

. . . .

Dear Father, I feel so lonely. It seems like everyone is against me, like no one cares anything about me. My head knows that's not true, but my emotions get the best of me. I'm so grateful for this promise that You are for me. You are always on my side. No matter what, You love me and You'll never leave me. And if You are for me, I'm always on the winning side. If You are with me, I'm never alone. When loneliness steals my joy, remind me of Your presence. Remind me of Your love. Whisper Your promises into my spirit. Help me shine Your light to others so no one else has to feel lonely. Thank You for always being on my team.

Be gracious to me, for I am lonely and afflicted.
PSALM 25:16 NIV

. . . .

Dear Father, I have lots of acquaintances. People know who I am, and most of them are nice to me. But I don't have anyone to share my secrets with. There's no one to text or call when something funny happens, no one to reach out to when I'm depressed, and no one to hang out with on weekends. I see other people in their groups—laughing, talking, fitting in—and I really want to be a part of that. I don't have to be Miss Popularity. I just want one or two people who get me, who like me, and who want to be around me. Will You please send me some good friends, who love You and will love me too? Thank You for never leaving me alone, even when I feel lonely.

A defender of widows, is God in his holy dwelling. God sets the lonely in families, he leads out the prisoners with singing; but the rebellious live in a sun-scorched land.
PSALM 68:5–6 NIV

. . . .

Dear Father, I have a family, but I still feel alone. I feel like no one understands me, and I don't feel connected to them in a deep friendship way. But I know feelings aren't always accurate. Help me give my family the benefit of the doubt. Maybe they understand more than I think they do. Could You help me reach out, or let them reach out to me, so I don't feel so lonely? Could You send other people who will love me and accept me like family? Show me what I can do to cross this bridge from loneliness to togetherness. Lead me to others who need what I can give. Help me reach out so I can help someone else feel less lonely.

One who has unreliable friends soon comes to ruin, but there is a friend who sticks closer than a brother.
PROVERBS 18:24 NIV

. . . .

Dear Father, I have lots of people who claim to be my friends, but they don't feel like friends to me. I can't trust them to encourage me, protect me, and take care of me the way friends should. Even when we're together, I feel alone. But I know You are with me. I know You're always on my side, walking beside me, holding my hand, encouraging me, and building me up. I know I can talk to You about anything, and You'll love me the same. Thank You for loving me that way. Give me the courage to distance myself from people who make me feel lonely, even in a crowd. Connect me with others who will be true friends. And make me that kind of friend to others as well.

Where can I go from your Spirit? Where can I flee from your presence? If I go up to the heavens, you are there; if I make my bed in the depths, you are there.
PSALM 139:7–8 NIV

• •

Dear Father, sometimes the loneliness in my heart feels so deep, so bottomless, that I feel like I'll never find my way out. I long for true friendship, for a real connection with someone, but there's no one. Yet, I know I'm never truly alone, am I? The King of kings, Creator of the universe, almighty and all-powerful God wants to spend time with me. You never leave me for even a second. When I'm sad, You're there. When I'm excited, You're there. When something great happens, You celebrate with me, whispering in my ear that You're proud of me. Thank You for that kind of fierce love. When I think of You, I don't feel so alone.

MOVING

"Remember not the former things, nor consider the things of old. Behold, I am doing a new thing; now it springs forth, do you not perceive it? I will make a way in the wilderness and rivers in the desert."
ISAIAH 43:18–19 ESV

. . . .

Dear Father, I know I'm supposed to look ahead, not behind. I know You have good things in store for my future. But moving is hard. I have to say goodbye to everyone and everything that's familiar. I have so many memories here. My friends, my school, my whole identity is wrapped up in this place. Help me hold these sweet memories close. At the same time, fill me with excitement for what lies ahead. Lead me to new friends who will encourage me and help me live for You. Open up new doors and amazing opportunities. Most of all, help me carry Your light into this unfamiliar place.

Trust in the LORD with all your heart, and
do not lean on your own understanding.
In all your ways acknowledge him, and
he will make straight your paths.
PROVERBS 3:5–6 ESV

. . . .

Dear Father, it's hard to trust You when I don't know what lies ahead. I guess that's the whole purpose of trust, isn't it? It's believing that You love me, You'll take care of me, and You have good things in store for my life. Right now, this move doesn't make sense to me. I don't understand why I have to leave my home, my friends, my church, and my school. I'm comfortable here, and I hate the thought of starting over. Even when I leave all those behind, I know You'll never leave me. I'll look to You and trust You to show me the way. Thank You for walking with me into the unknown.

Brothers, I do not consider that I have made it my own. But one thing I do: forgetting what lies behind and straining forward to what lies ahead, I press on toward the goal for the prize of the upward call of God in Christ Jesus.
PHILIPPIANS 3:13–14 ESV

. . . .

Dear Father, right now, I don't want to look ahead. Thinking about the future just gives me anxiety. I have no idea what's in store. I'd rather stay right here where I'm comfortable, where I have friends, where I'm known and loved. What if I can't find new friends? What if I hate my new home, my new school? Help me set aside my fears. I know my entire life will be a series of changes. Wherever I'm at on the journey, You want my focus to be on what's ahead. Hold my hand, and help me walk into this unknown future with confidence.

Therefore, since we are surrounded by
so great a cloud of witnesses, let us also
lay aside every weight, and sin which
clings so closely, and let us run with
endurance the race that is set before us.
HEBREWS 12:1 ESV

Dear Father, I know I'm not the first person who's had to move. I know it's normal to feel anxiety in this situation. That great cloud of witnesses in this verse is people who lived before me, who loved You and followed You. Many of them had to endure a whole lot worse than I'm facing. But every one of them endured. They made it through, and I can too. I know this race I'm running has many exciting things in store, and I'll never experience them if I don't move forward. Hold my hand. Calm my fears. Run this race with me, Father. I need You by my side.

OVERWHELMED

When my anxious thoughts multiply within me, Your comfort delights my soul.
PSALM 94:19 NASB

. . . .

Dear Father, the words in this verse perfectly describe how I feel. My anxious thoughts create more anxious thoughts, and my worries multiply until they consume me. I feel smothered and choked, my stomach is in tangles, and I'm frozen in fear. I don't have any idea how to start fighting my way out of this place. But when I take my eyes off my circumstances and focus on You, my breathing calms down and gets deeper. I feel Your peace. I hear You whisper, "Be still." And I know that, no matter what, You'll see me through this time. There is no problem too big for You, no pit too deep for You to pull me out. There is nothing too hard for You, and You're right here with me, fighting for me. Thank You for comforting me and reminding me of Your love.

*Hear my cry, God; give Your attention
to my prayer. From the end of the earth
I call to You when my heart is faint; lead
me to the rock that is higher than I.*
PSALM 61:1–2 NASB

. . . .

Dear Father, I am overwhelmed. Right now, my circumstances seem too much for me. I can't carry it all, and I just want to quit everything and hide. Will You please help me through this? Show me the next step. Just one step, Lord, and then another and another. Hold my hand and lead me out of this hard place, to a place where I can breathe and smile and be happy again. Take my anxiety and trade it for Your peace. When I focus on my problems, they seem like giants. But when I focus on You, my troubles seem small in comparison. Thank You for being bigger than my problems and thank You for guiding me through this hard time.

Yet those who wait for the LORD will gain new strength; they will mount up with wings like eagles, they will run and not get tired, they will walk and not become weary.
ISAIAH 40:31 NASB

. . . .

Dear Father, I don't like my circumstances right now. So many things are happening, and I feel like my life is closing in on me. My first response is to fight against it all. I want to jump ahead of You and make things happen on my timeline. But You want me to wait. You want me to relax and trust You. That's hard for me, Lord. Patience does not come easily for me. But whenever I try to do it on my own, without trusting You, things don't turn out well. Help me calm my spirit. Help me wait for Your perfect timing. I know You have a good plan for my life and that Your way is always better than mine.

I will raise my eyes to the mountains; from where will my help come? My help comes from the LORD, who made heaven and earth.
PSALM 121:1–2 NASB

. . . .

Dear Father, I need help right now. I'm overwhelmed. So many things are happening at once, and I don't feel capable of dealing with it all. Anxiety steals my breath, and worry robs me of sleep. Will You help me? Will You show me what I need to do first, second, third? Clear my mind so I can focus. Give me wisdom to know how to proceed. And give me confidence in Your guidance. I don't know what to do, so I'm going to do nothing. I'll stand right here and listen for Your voice. I will act when I hear Your instructions. Speak to me, Lord. Give me direction, and show me the way. Thank You for helping me.

The name of the LORD is a strong tower;
the righteous runs into it and is safe.
PROVERBS 18:10 NASB

. . . .

Dear Father, I feel chased right now. It seems like life is pursuing me, closing in on me, and there's no place to hide. But I know that no matter where I am or what I'm going through, I can always run to You. You're always there, arms open wide, waiting to scoop me up into the safety of Your love. Here I am, running to You. I'm desperate for You, Lord. Let me feel Your presence and breathe in Your peace. Let me hear Your voice and soak in Your kindness. Calm my heart. Protect me from harm. Give me confidence in Your power. Thank You for taking care of me even in the worst of times. Instead of being overwhelmed by my fears, I want to be overwhelmed by Your love.

REGRET

Godly sorrow brings repentance that
leads to salvation and leaves no regret,
but worldly sorrow brings death.
2 CORINTHIANS 7:10 NIV

Dear Father, I have some pretty big regrets. I wish I had done things differently, made different choices, and handled situations in a better way. I wish there were a way to rewind time and take back things I said and did, but there's not. I guess the best thing I can do at this point is try to learn from my mistakes and not repeat them. If those regrets make me wiser, kinder, and more compassionate, I guess they've served a purpose. If my mistakes help me really look at myself, and ultimately help me become a more godly person, then they're worth it. I guess that's one way You cause things to work together for our good, isn't it? Use my past mistakes to make me more like You.

Do not say, "Why were the old days better than these?" For it is not wise to ask such questions.
ECCLESIASTES 7:10 NIV

. . . .

Dear Father, Solomon wrote these words, and he's considered the wisest man in history. It's easy to look at the past through a rose-colored filter. I have a selective memory, and I see what I want to recall instead of remembering the truth of how things were. That kind of recollection leads me to be dissatisfied with my current life. I think, "If only I'd made a different choice, things would still be like they were." The truth is, You want me to look forward. I can't relive the past; I can only learn from it. Help me look ahead with excitement and anticipation of the great things You'll do in my life. I know You have good things in store for me. I trust You completely.

"I will repay you for the years the locusts have eaten—the great locust and the young locust, the other locusts and the locust swarm— my great army that I sent among you."
JOEL 2:25 NIV

Dear Father, I look at my life and how it's turned out, and I feel like so much time has been lost or wasted with sadness, anger, and negativity. Why do things have to be so hard? You said You want us to have abundant life. So far, my life hasn't felt very abundant. But in this verse, You promise to repay the years the locusts have eaten. You promise to restore what has been lost. From this point forward, will You restore? Will You let me experience some of the joy You promised those who love You? Even though I've been through hard things, I trust in Your goodness. I know You have amazing, beautiful, wonderful things waiting in my future.

I have fought the good fight, I have finished the race, I have kept the faith.
2 TIMOTHY 4:7 NIV

. . . .

Dear Father, I don't want my life to be a fight. But that's what it feels like, and I'm tired. I've made so many mistakes, so many bad choices, and they've led me down a road I don't want to travel. But I know this road I'm on is just part of the journey. It's not the destination. The regrets I have are part of the process, and they're shaping me into the person I'll become. I don't want to repeat my mistakes. Instead, I want to learn and grow from them. When I get to the end of my life, I don't want to have regrets. I want to be able to look back and see that each step brought me closer to becoming the person You created me to be.

And the God of all grace, who called you to his eternal glory in Christ, after you have suffered a little while, will himself restore you and make you strong, firm and steadfast.
1 PETER 5:10 NIV

. . . .

Dear Father, I know life is a journey filled with hills and valleys. But it seems like I've been in the valley for a long time. I've made choices I regret. I've done things I wish I could undo. Right now, I'm suffering the consequences of bad decisions. I know the suffering is part of the process, but I'm asking You to help me through it. Teach me what I need to learn. Help me move out of this valley and into a better place in my life. Most importantly, I don't want to repeat the mistakes that led me to this place. Teach me, mold me, and make me like You.

RESPONSIBILITIES

*Now we who are strong ought to bear the
weaknesses of those without strength,
and not just please ourselves.*
ROMANS 15:1 NASB

. . . .

Dear Father, it's not fair that I have to work
when others don't do their share. Why should I
have to carry the load? I'm still young. I should
be enjoying myself like other kids my age. But I
know that's not the right attitude. I know You've
made me strong and capable, and I should view
it as an honor to be able to help out and serve
others. Change my attitude, Lord. I don't want
to resent the responsibilities I have. Help me
view everything I do as a way to honor You. Give
me joy in each task. Help me do everything well.
And help me accomplish the things I need to
do so I can relax some too.

"The one who is faithful in a very little thing is also faithful in much; and the one who is unrighteous in a very little thing is also unrighteous in much."
LUKE 16:10 NASB

Dear Father, I know the little things are important. But some of the things I have to do seem so insignificant and pointless. If I have to work, why can't I do something more important and exciting? Yet, I know that if I don't do the little insignificant things, they probably won't get done. And if they don't get done, everyone will suffer. As I complete each task with excellence, I grow in my skill and ability, and I increase the chances of being given more responsibility. Make me a hard worker. Help me stop complaining. Teach me to find joy in even the little things. In all I do, I want to honor You.

"Instead, brothers and sisters, select from among you seven men of good reputation, full of the Spirit and of wisdom, whom we may put in charge of this task."
ACTS 6:3 NASB

• •

Dear Father, I want to be chosen. I want to be one of the important ones, in charge of the important jobs. But I have to ask myself if I fit the qualifications listed here for those who were chosen. Do I have a good reputation? Do I work hard, with a smile on my face, or do I avoid work and complain about it when I'm forced? Am I full of Your wisdom, or do I do foolish things that put myself and others at risk? Make me a hard worker, Father. Make me wise and kind and loving. Help me act in a way that leads to a good reputation. Make me like You.

So they are to perform the duties of the tent of meeting, the holy place, and of assisting the sons of Aaron their relatives, for the service of the house of the LORD.
1 CHRONICLES 23:32 NASB

. . . .

Dear Father, there weren't any stars in this show, were there? The entire group worked together, each doing the task assigned to him in order to take care of the holy place. Each one had a set of jobs, and if one of them didn't do his job, someone else had to take up the slack. Make me like these workers. Help me quietly complete my responsibilities without needing recognition or special treatment. When someone else needs help, remind me to give it without complaint or judgment. I want to be a hard worker and a responsible person. I know that's the kind of person You created me to be.

SELF-ESTEEM

Then God said, "Let us make man in our image, after our likeness. And let them have dominion over the fish of the sea and over the birds of the heavens and over the livestock and over all the earth and over every creeping thing that creeps on the earth."
GENESIS 1:26 ESV

. . . .

Dear Father, sometimes I question my value. I wonder what I'm good for, what I have to contribute to this world. I compare myself to other people, and I usually come up short. But You made me in Your image. You made me to be like You, yet different from every other human on the planet. I know You wouldn't have created me without a purpose. I have value because I'm Yours. Help me see my worth, and help me love and encourage others so they can know their value as well.

*But you are a chosen race, a royal
priesthood, a holy nation, a people for his
own possession, that you may proclaim
the excellencies of him who called you out
of darkness into his marvelous light.*
1 PETER 2:9 ESV

. . . .

Dear Father, sometimes I'm the last one chosen
for things, or I'm not chosen at all. But You chose
me. You say I'm royalty because I'm Your child.
You call me holy, which means set aside for a
special purpose. My job is to be Your ambassador here on earth. The dictionary defines an
ambassador as "an official of the highest rank,
sent by one sovereign or state to another to
represent it on a temporary mission." I'm Your
representative, and that's an important job. Help
me hold my head high and represent You well
as I love others, show kindness and compassion,
and do what is right. That is where I find my
purpose and value.

"No longer do I call you servants, for the servant does not know what his master is doing; but I have called you friends, for all that I have heard from my Father I have made known to you."
JOHN 15:15 ESV

. . . .

Dear Father, sometimes I feel like an outcast. I want to have friends and be part of a group, but I don't fit in. Yet, You made me part of Your in-crowd. You call me Your friend, and that's pretty amazing. You chose me and made me Your daughter. Help me focus less on what others think of me and more on what they think of You. Instead of worrying about whether people *like* me, I want to make sure they know they are loved. Help me show kindness in a world that's not kind. Help me encourage when others tear down. Thank You for calling me Your friend. I want to show others what a great friend You are.

But now thus says the LORD, he who created you, O Jacob, he who formed you, O Israel: "Fear not, for I have redeemed you; I have called you by name, you are mine."
ISAIAH 43:1 ESV

. . . .

Dear Father, I know You've called me by name. I feel Your presence, even when no one is around. I feel Your love, even when the world is harsh. And when I'm an outcast, when I don't belong anywhere, You say I belong to You. Thank You for giving me value and worth. Help me live up to the value You've placed on me. I'm a daughter of the King, so help me behave like one. Remind me to hold my head up and my shoulders back. Remind me to smile at people. When I feel lonely or rejected, help me reach out to someone else who looks like an outcast. I want to build others' sense of worth the way You've built mine.

*"Because you are precious in my eyes, and
honored, and I love you, I give men in return
for you, peoples in exchange for your life."*
Isaiah 43:4 esv

. . . .

Dear Father, am I really precious to You? Am I
honored? Do You really love me like this verse
says You do? Deep down, I know I can trust these
words. In my spirit, I hear You whisper that I'm
Yours and that You love me more than Your own
life. When I feel down on myself, remind me not
to find my worth in what others think of me, or
even in what I think of myself. My worth is found
in You. Your Word is final, and You've chosen
to love me. Like any royal child, I am valuable
not because of who I am but because of who
my Father is. Today and every day, I choose to
love You back.

SEX

*Flee sexual immorality. Every other
sin that a person commits is outside
the body, but the sexually immoral
person sins against his own body.*
1 CORINTHIANS 6:18 NASB

. . . .

Dear Father, so many people I know treat sexual sin like it's no big deal. They act like it's silly and old-fashioned to wait for marriage. But I know You love me, and Your guidelines are given out of love. When we share our bodies with another person sexually, we become physically intimate with that person. We fully give ourselves to them. Then, when that person leaves us or doesn't appreciate the risk we took to share that kind of intimacy, it hurts. So many negative consequences come from having sex outside of marriage the way You designed it. I know You don't want us to be hurt. Help me stand strong in my convictions. I trust the motives behind Your guidelines, even when those around me don't understand.

But because of sexual immoralities, each man is to have his own wife, and each woman is to have her own husband.
1 CORINTHIANS 7:2 NASB

. . . .

Dear Father, sex isn't bad, is it? It's a good thing, in the proper place and time. It's kind of like swimsuits—they're great at the beach, but they're not the best attire for snow skiing. Sex, in the right context, is great. But it's hard to live in a world where people think it's fine to have sex with anyone, outside of marriage. It's also hard when sex is easy to find in movies and on social media, and they make it look fantastic. Yet, I'm not supposed to participate— even though everyone else is and they look like they're enjoying it. When I'm tempted to compromise my standards, remind me that sin has consequences. Help me not to fill my mind with images that make me question my values. And remind me to be patient and wait for the right time to enjoy sex.

*But sexual immorality or any impurity
or greed must not even be mentioned
among you, as is proper among saints.*
EPHESIANS 5:3 NASB

. . . .

Dear Father, sexual immorality, by Your standards, is everywhere. It's even in the church. It's almost as common among my Christian friends as it is among non-Christians. When I hold strong to my convictions, others make fun of me, laugh behind my back, and call me a prude. Please send me some friends who want to remain pure, Father. It's easier to make the right choices when I'm not the only one. Help me not to come across as preachy or judgmental to others who have made different choices. Instead, help me love others the way You love them and show them that following You leads to long-term joy, peace, and fulfillment. Give me wisdom, strength, and conviction to follow You even when others don't.

For this reason a man shall leave his father and his mother, and be joined to his wife; and they shall become one flesh.
GENESIS 2:24 NASB

. . . .

Dear Father, in Your Word, You're very clear about when and where we're supposed to be sexually intimate. A husband and wife, joined together in marriage, have Your blessing for this kind of relationship. It's not wrong to want this kind of intimacy. You created us for it! But Satan loves to take the good things You created and turn them into something dirty and harmful. When we give ourselves in this way to people we haven't committed to and who haven't committed to us in marriage, we risk getting hurt. Thank You for giving us guidelines, and for saving some things just for the most intimate of relationships. Forgive me for my past mistakes in this area, and keep me pure in the future.

Therefore, treat the parts of your earthly body as dead to sexual immorality, impurity, passion, evil desire, and greed, which amounts to idolatry.

COLOSSIANS 3:5 NASB

. . . .

Dear Father, sex inside the boundaries of a healthy marriage is not dirty or wrong or immoral, but having sex outside of marriage takes something You intended to be safe and fun and makes it dangerous. When I'm tempted to jump into sexual immorality, hold me back. Keep me safe. And give me strength to say no when others pressure me to do things I know aren't in Your perfect plan for my life.

SHAME

"I advise you to buy from Me gold refined by fire so that you may become rich, and white garments so that you may clothe yourself and the shame of your nakedness will not be revealed; and eye salve to apply to your eyes so that you may see."
REVELATION 3:18 NASB

. . . .

Dear Father, I am a sinner. I have every reason to be ashamed, apart from Christ. But in Christ, I find every good thing, and I can hold my head high. Without Him, I'm poor, but with Him, I'm rich. Without Him, I'm stripped bare with only rags, but with Him, I'm clothed in beautiful white robes. Without Him, I'm blind to so many things, but Christ opens my eyes so I can see and understand things that are above me. Thank You for loving me, dying for me, and taking away my shame. I'll hold my head high, not because of who I am alone but because of who I am in You.

For this is contained in Scripture: "Behold, I am laying in Zion a choice stone, a precious cornerstone, and the one who believes in Him will not be put to shame."
1 PETER 2:6 NASB

. . . .

Dear Father, a cornerstone is the strong, foundational stone that supports all the other stones or bricks in a building. The cornerstone has to be the strongest, straightest, and truest. Jesus is that precious cornerstone. I may not be much on my own, but I believe in Jesus. It's more than a head knowledge. I believe in my heart that He is Your Son and that He took my shame on the cross so I wouldn't have to. He has changed my life. Thank You for sending Your Son to pay for my sins. When I feel ashamed of my life or my past, remind me that it's all been paid for. It's all been erased. I have nothing to feel shame for because Jesus took it from me.

*But God has chosen the foolish things
of the world to shame the wise, and God
has chosen the weak things of the world
to shame the things which are strong.*
1 CORINTHIANS 1:27 NASB

. . . .

Dear Father, I know You don't see me as foolish or weak. But others do. It feels awful when others look down on me, laugh at me, and talk about me behind my back. They may see me as foolish, but as long as I follow You, I am wise. In some ways, I may be weak. But through You, I am stronger than I ever thought possible. Help me hold my head high, love others even when they don't love me, and shine Your light in this dark world. I'd rather be a fool for You than respected without You. Do with me as You will, Lord. I'm Yours.

According to my eager expectation and hope, that I will not be put to shame in anything, but that with all boldness, Christ will even now, as always, be exalted in my body, whether by life or by death.
PHILIPPIANS 1:20 NASB

. . . .

Dear Father, if anyone had reason to be ashamed, it was Paul. Before he met Christ, he persecuted Christians. It was Paul (formerly known as Saul) who gave approval for the mob to stone Stephen, the first Christian martyr. But You changed everything, didn't You? You forgave Paul's past, set him on a new path, and gave him a fresh start. Because of what You did, Paul ended up writing much of the New Testament. His work changed countless lives. I know You're giving me a fresh start too. I'm Yours, Lord. Set me on a new path. Like Paul, I want You to use my life to glorify You.

*"Fear not, for you will not be put to shame;
and do not feel humiliated, for you will not
be disgraced; but you will forget the shame
of your youth, and no longer remember
the disgrace of your widowhood."*

ISAIAH 54:4 NASB

. . . .

Dear Father, You're in the business of giving fresh starts and new beginnings. I feel so ashamed of things I've done. But I've said I'm sorry for those things, and I can't go back and change my past. When shameful thoughts seep in, remind me that I'm not the same person anymore. You've wiped the slate clean, and You'll find ways to use my experiences to point others to You. I pray You will help me forget the bad parts of my past. I know those things are nothing but a shadow compared to Your light. Thank You for loving me enough to clean me off, set me on a new path, and make something beautiful of my life.

THE FUTURE

The mind of a person plans his way,
but the LORD directs his steps.
PROVERBS 16:9 NASB

. . . .

Dear Father, I have plans for my life. Big plans. I have so many dreams and goals and ambitions. I hope some of them come true, but I know there's a good chance all of them won't. That's okay, because I know my future is in Your hands. I know You love me, and You've already mapped out a path for my life. That path includes making me into the woman You want me to be. It includes loving people and showing them who You are. And it includes blessings and treasures more amazing than anything I could dream up. Thank You for directing my steps. You know my plans, Lord. But following You is more important to me than anything. No matter what life brings, I will trust You.

Come now, you who say, "Today or tomorrow we will go to such and such a city, and spend a year there and engage in business and make a profit." Yet you do not know what your life will be like tomorrow. For you are just a vapor that appears for a little while, and then vanishes away. Instead, you ought to say, "If the Lord wills, we will live and also do this or that."
JAMES 4:13–15 NASB

. . . .

Dear Father, I like to dream about the future. In those dreams, everything works out just like I want. But I know I can't rely on my plans. My future will bring both blessing and hardship. The only thing I can rely on completely is Your love for me. You know my dreams, my hopes, and my desires, but I trust Your plan for my life. I know You have good things in store for me.

Many plans are in a person's heart,
but the advice of the LORD will stand.
PROVERBS 19:21 NASB

. . . .

Dear Father, when I think of the future, I have so many plans. I will be successful and loved and happy. I love to daydream about the perfect version of how my life will turn out, but I know my hopes and dreams are nothing compared to the grand adventure You have waiting for me. When my ideas conflict with Your plans for my life, help me set aside *my* plans and follow You. When ambition pulls me away from You, draw me back. Hold me close, and don't let me wander too far. More than anything, I want to become the person You created me to be. I want to live out Your purpose for my life. Show me the path You want me to take, Lord. I will follow You.

"The LORD your God is in your midst,
a victorious warrior. He will rejoice over
you with joy, He will be quiet in His love,
He will rejoice over you with shouts of joy."
ZEPHANIAH 3:17 NASB

. . . .

Dear Father, what's in store for my future? Here I am, at the front part of my life, and there are so many different paths to choose from. I don't know which ones to take, and I'm afraid I'll make the wrong choice. But I know that You're right here with me and that You'll always help me when I ask. Give me wisdom. Guide me and show me the way You want me to go. No matter what, I want to please You. I want to go where You are because that is where I'll experience the love, joy, and abundant life You promised to those who follow You.

"Do not be afraid, little flock, because your Father has chosen to give you the kingdom."
LUKE 12:32 NASB

. . . .

Dear Father, when I think of the future, I get anxious. I'm afraid of what's in store. What if I make a wrong choice? What if something bad happens? I wish I could see what's ahead. But when it comes to the future, You only light the way a little at a time. Help me not to worry about what's down the road. All I need to do is take the next step—the one You've shown me. When I get there, I'll take the next step and the next. If I don't know what to do, I'll stand still until You direct me. I'll trust You, and I won't be afraid. I know You have a wonderful, exciting adventure planned, and You have good things in store for my life.

UNFORGIVENESS

"And when you stand praying, if you hold anything against anyone, forgive them, so that your Father in heaven may forgive you your sins."
MARK 11:25 NIV

• •

Dear Father, I know I'm supposed to forgive those who hurt me. I just don't know how. Am I supposed to forget what they did? Am I supposed to say it's okay? Because what they did isn't okay, and no matter how hard I try, I can't forget it. I'm not like You. I don't have the ability to just remove something from my mind and wipe the record clean. Help me understand. Show me what forgiveness looks like. I need to learn *two things*: forgiveness, which lets someone off the hook for past mistakes, and wisdom, which puts up healthy boundaries so a person doesn't keep hurting me. I need Your help here, Father. Show me how to truly forgive.

"For if you forgive other people when they sin against you, your heavenly Father will also forgive you. But if you do not forgive others their sins, your Father will not forgive your sins."
MATTHEW 6:14–15 NIV

. . . .

Dear Father, I'm learning about forgiveness the hard way. I still carry around the pain that others caused me, and it's difficult to pretend the pain isn't real. But forgiveness doesn't mean justice isn't done. Forgiveness doesn't mean the person won't be held accountable. It just means I'm letting go of the problem and giving it to You. I'm not in charge of justice or revenge. I can let it go and trust that, in Your way and Your time, justice will happen. Help me forgive, Father. It doesn't come easy. But when I think of how You have forgiven me for all the ways I've hurt You, I know I have to forgive others.

Be kind and compassionate to one another, forgiving each other, just as in Christ God forgave you.
EPHESIANS 4:32 NIV

. . . .

Dear Father, when I mess up, I want others to go easy on me. But when others mess up, it really gets on my nerves. I don't know why I'm so moody and irritable, but I'm having a hard time showing patience with others. Calm my spirit. Make me generous and compassionate and kind. I know those aren't traits that will just miraculously show up. They're qualities I have to perfect over time with lots of practice. I need Your help with this, Lord. When others do things that upset me, help me take some deep breaths and act with patience, even if I don't feel patient. Help me act with kindness, even if I don't feel kind. And help me forgive others the way I want them to forgive me.

*"In your anger do not sin": Do not let the
sun go down while you are still angry,
and do not give the devil a foothold.*
EPHESIANS 4:26–27 NIV

. . . .

Dear Father, it's easy to sin when I'm angry. I say things I shouldn't, and I hold a grudge against the person who made me mad. But that's not how You want me to behave, is it? You want me to forgive others, even when they make me angry. This verse reminds me that anger is an emotion, and it's not wrong to feel angry. It is wrong to lose my temper. It is wrong to say hurtful things to others. It is wrong to plan revenge. One way I can avoid sin, even when I'm angry, is to think of all the times You've forgiven me even though I probably frustrated You. Teach me to be angry and not sin. Teach me to forgive.

"So watch yourselves. If your brother or sister sins against you, rebuke them; and if they repent, forgive them. Even if they sin against you seven times in a day and seven times come back to you saying 'I repent,' you must forgive them."
LUKE 17:3–4 NIV

. . . .

Dear Father, it's easy enough to say I forgive someone, but it's hard to remove the memories from my mind. Every time I recall the pain they caused, I feel hurt all over again. I want to forgive, but it's hard to let go when I have to relive it again and again in my mind. Help me treat each of those recollections as an opportunity to forgive a little more. Each time a hurtful memory comes to mind, help me breathe in forgiveness and breathe out the pain. Eventually, as I forgive that person enough, my heart will heal. I know forgiveness does more for me than for the other person. Thank You for helping me forgive.